189528

SCOTLAND'S PAST IN ACTION

D1350838

LIBREX

Falkirk Council

Other titles in the series are *Spinning and Weaving, Farming, Fishing and Whaling, Sporting Scotland, Making Cars, Building Railways, Feeding Scotland, Leaving Scotland, Going to School, Going to Church* and *Going on Holiday*.

Published by NMS Publishing, Chambers Street, Edinburgh EHI IJF

© Trustees of the National Museums of Scotland 1997

Series Editor Iseabail Macleod

British Library Cataloguing in Publication Data

A catalogue record of this book is available from the British Library

ISBN 0 948636 92 0

Designed by NMS Publishing

Printed in Great Britain by BPC Wheatons Ltd, Exeter

Acknowledgements

Many people helped to find the the the material for this book: Dr Malcolm Bangor-Jones, George Dalgleish, Professor Sandy Fenton, Antonia Ineson, Iseabail Macleod, Andrew Martin, Liz Robertson, Dr Allen Simpson, Gavin Sprott, Elaine Thomson, and Robin Urquhart. I am deeply grateful to them all.

Illustrations: Front cover, iii bottom, 44, 47, 48, 67: Lothian Health Board Archives. Back cover, ii top, iii top: Liz Robertson. i, 4, 8, 11, 12, 16, 21, 22, 23, 27, 30, 33, 39, 41, 43, 45, 50, 54, 59, 62, 63, 64, 69, 72, 76, 77, 80: National Museums of Scotland. ii bottom, 10, 35: John Burnett. iv top: Scottish National Portrait Gallery. iv bottom: Scotsman Publications. 38, 57: Glasgow City Archives. 58: Eric Simpson. 61: Northern Health Services Archives. 65: Medical Photography, Royal Infirmary, Edinburgh. 71: Miss E Strong. 73, 74: Health Promotion Department, Lothian Health. 78: Professor John Mallard.

Illustrations captioned SLA are from the Scottish Life Archive in the National Museums of Scotland.

Front cover: *A calendar sold to raise money for the Royal Edinburgh Hospital for Sick Children, 1934.*

Back cover: *The statue of Hygeia (1788) at St Bernard's Well beside the Water of Leith, Edinburgh.*

CONTENTS

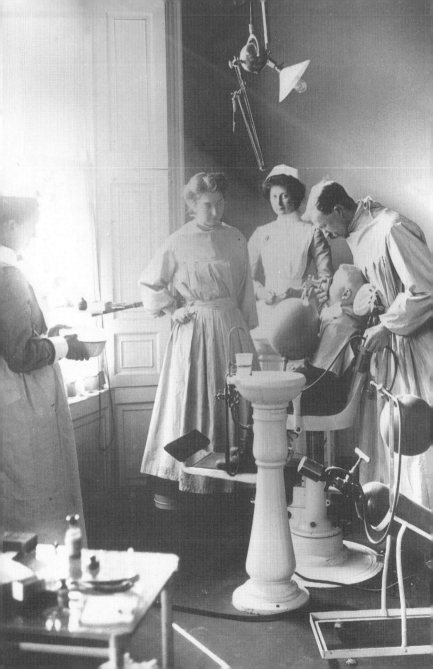

INTRODUCTION

Illness is a natural part of childhood, a common experience for adults, and an almost inevitable part of old age. The poet William Dunbar began his great 'Lament for the Makars', for his fellow-poets lately dead:

> I that in heill wes and gladnes,   [health]
> Am trublit now with gret siekness
> And feblit with infermite;
> > *Timor mortis conturbat me.*

I am ill and weak: the fear of death disturbs me. Dunbar died in 1520: he had been at the lively and cultured court of James IV. Yet disease was ever-present and life was short. When war intervened it affected all social classes – 'the Floors o the Forest' were cut down at Flodden in 1513 – and those who were not killed on the battlefield often died after infection entered their wounds. Epidemic disease was rife; the Black Death which swept north-wards over Scotland in 1349-50 killed more than one third of the population of Europe. Illness is always with us, as a vivid memory or a shadowy terror. Dunbar recognized the limits of the power of the doctor:

> In medicyne the most practicianis,
> Lechis, surrigianis, and phisicianis,
> Thame self fra ded may not supple   [help]
> > *Timor mortis conturbat me.*

At the same time, people were completely aware – in a way that few of us are today – of the natural world around them and of

A child being anaesthetized before having a tooth extracted, Edinburgh, about 1914. SLA

themselves as part of it. Man was an animal, and the understanding of the health of one linked with knowledge of the other. A proverb says, 'Ye hae skeil o man an baest – ye was born atween the Beltanes'. A child born between pagan Beltane and its Christian cousin the invention or discovery of the Cross, that is between 1 and 3 May, was said to have powers which could be applied to all members of the living world.

This book is not a history of medical triumph, of scientific discoveries and lives saved. Rather, it is about the place of health and sickness in the lives of the Scots, about the ways in which illness has been seen – a pattern of hopes and fears, caring and indifference. Triumphs there have been, certainly, when science enabled doctors to understand, cure and prevent disease, but failures there have been by the thousand, every time knowledge has been unable to avoid the shortening of a life. Or was it failure? Illness and death are as natural as life.

The history of medicine is a vast field and touches on many aspects of our lives. I have restricted this account in five ways. First, I focus on events in Scotland only, though something has to be said of discoveries elsewhere to make sense of the Scottish story. Second, I begin with the last great famine, the 'seven ill years' of the 1690s, leaving aside prehistoric, medieval and early modern medicine. This means that some fascinating subjects have had to be omitted, such as recent archaeological discoveries at the medieval hospital at Soutra in Lothian and in the graveyard at Whithorn in Galloway. Third, I have balanced an account of progress in medicine with a description of the choices of kinds of medicine which people felt they had, whether in sickness they went to a folk practitioner, perhaps illiterate, or a university graduate. Fourth, I have written about health as well as about medicine, looking at issues to do with diet and public health. Finally, I have stressed the material side of medicine, the use of fleams for bloodletting, the development of instruments for diagnosis in the nineteenth century, and of new kinds of drugs and of 'high-tech' medicine in the twentieth.

Nevertheless, health and medicine are such large subjects that there are many topics which have been left out. The growth of the professions of nursing and midwifery, of medical education and specialization, of the pharmaceutical industry and its vast research effort, of medical publishing – all these subjects deserve a coverage which they have not received here – as do different theories of disease, psychiatry and mental illness, alternative and complementary medicine. The idea that dependency on alcohol was an illness was developed in the eighteenth century by a Scot, Thomas Trotter, a contemporary of the great anatomists William and John Hunter, brothers born in East Kilbride, who made their careers in London. This is the only time these individuals are mentioned in this book. There is also a local aspect to medicine, for each town had its own particular experiences – say, of the great cholera epidemic of 1832-3 – and the story of each hospital relates in its own way to its local context.

Edinburgh occupies a leading place in this account because of the pre-eminence of its medical school and the presence of many important figures there. Medical progress has been made largely in cities, and until the twentieth century remote parts of the country were remote from practitioners with formal medical training: people lived and died in the world of folk medicine. Now a sick man, or a woman in labour in the Western or Northern Isles may travel to hospital by air while a city dweller can walk there. Modern medicine reaches us everywhere.

1 The ill years

Some Die by the Way-side, some drop down in the Street, the poor sucking Babs are Starving for want of Milk, which the empty Breasts of their Mothers cannot furnish them: Every one may see Death in the Face of the Poor, that abound every where; the Thinness of their Visage, their ghostly looks, their Feebleness, their Agues [fevers] & their fluxes [diarrhoea] threaten them with sudden Death.

For several years around 1690 there had been abundant harvests and corn was cheap. Political power changed hands: King James VII fled, and William of Orange routed his soldiers despite the victory-in-death of James Graham of Claverhouse at Killie-crankie. Of more vital importance was the fact that the people had food. Then came three bad harvests in succession (1693-5) and the stocks of grain were exhausted. A crisis was beginning.

In the winter of 1694-5 poor people died in the streets of Leith. The following winter ordinary folk reduced to begging flooded into Edinburgh, and the town made a camp for them in Greyfriars churchyard. This was the space into which the defeated Covenanters had been herded after the Battle of Rullion Green thirty years before; its choice as a kind of sanctuary was not a benevolent gesture. In the autumn the crops failed again in the south of Scotland that year and in view of 'the great dearth and tyme of scarcity' the town again fed the poor for three months. Most of them came from outside Edinburgh, and with the advent of spring were told to return to their parishes. Kirk Sessions recorded the deaths of unknown strangers, searching for food. In

Greyfriars Churchyard, Edinburgh, where a camp was made for the starving poor in the 1690s. Alasdair Alpin Macgregor Collection, SLA

Skeleton on a tomb in Marnoch churchyard, Aberdeenshire.

Glasgow there was a riot against the high price of grain. The harvest of 1697 was indifferent: there was no recovery of stocks of food, particularly of grain. The spring of 1698 was bitterly cold. In the parched summer only stunted crops grew from the little seed that had been available. The rain came in late summer, with gales; and the most meagre of harvests was completed only in January. 'All things look dismal here like the crope', wrote a minister near Glasgow. Edinburgh re-opened its camp for beggars. It was, a modern historian observed, 'the last old-fashioned subsistence crisis' in Scotland, the last full-scale failure of the food supply. The population fell by fifteen per cent in five years.

George Turnbull, minister of Alloa, noted in December 1698: 'this was a sad year among the commons the death continuing and increasing'. The under-fed were vulnerable to illness: it was disease, preying upon the weak, that was the killer. This was a dreadful time: these were 'King William's seven ill years', with the biblical flavour of Joseph in Egypt, and Old Testament retribution. The Burgh of Lanark appointed men to watch over the crops to ensure that none were stolen, and in Aberdeen and Elgin a guard patrolled at night to prevent the hungry from taking food.

What responses could be made? The one was theological. The seventeenth century had been intensely religious, when the kirk had exercised a severe discipline over the people; when injustice, torture, war and murder had been justified in the name of God. Now people prayed for deliverance and better weather; ironically, they fasted. Turnbull preached on Hosea 7.14, accusing his flock of ungodliness: 'And they have not cried unto me with their heart, when they howled upon their beds: they assemble themselves for corn and wine, and they rebel against me.' Lack of devotion had caused the famine, he said, and implied that in seven years of plenty the Scots had been insufficiently grateful.

Formal medicine had little to offer in the crisis. There were few doctors outside the larger towns: the educated physician was an urban creature. Elsewhere in Europe, a nobleman often had a medical man in his retinue, but not in impoverished Scotland. In as far as medical advice was available in the countryside of Lowland Scotland it came from the minister, the well-meaning laird and his wife who probably had a book or two to guide them, and from the bearers of traditional knowledge, wise women and skilful men. The position was different in the Gaelic-speaking world, as we will see in the next section.

The practical response to famine was given by Sir Robert Sibbald (1641-1722), doctor, polymath and religious sceptic. Edinburgh had been the second place in Britain to have a botanic garden and with its aid Sibbald prepared the Edinburgh *Pharmacopoeia* (1699), a major step forward in establishing the standard and effective use of drugs. Sibbald began his reflections

The silver brooch given to Sarah Livingstone, who nursed Sir Colin Campbell (1776-1847). Campbell served in the Peninsular War and was Governor of Ceylon.

Rhubarb, from John Parkinson's Theatrum Botanicum *(1640). It was used as a laxative.*

on famine, characteristically for the period, with a pious thought – that God had placed the Scots in the midst of a great variety of food – but he continued realistically, and encouraged them to alter their diet so that it used the plants and animals which were available. Some of his suggestions amounted to being aware that some sources of nourishment were only available for a short season – birds' eggs, strawberries – but others were useful all the time. He listed animals which might be eaten: the otter, moudewart [mole], squirrel, mertrick [pine marten], whittret [stoat], weasel, ferret, and 'the hinder legs of Paddocks [frogs] of a yellowish colour are eaten, & taste well & nourish'. 'A kitchen garden might be a means of extending the diet', but it was also 'a reserve for bad Years'.

Sibbald's pamphlet is strange in that it was written to save the poor from starvation, but contains references to ancient Roman authors: perhaps the patina of scholarship made his suggestions more convincing to the educated reader who would pass on ideas to the pauper. Sibbald was one of the most learned men of his generation, and used his wide reading to point out possible sources of food: the Chinese eat dogs, and the Faroe Islanders build wooden 'wind houses' to dry and thus preserve fish.

One consequence of the 'seven ill years' was an economic feebleness which made the idea of the Union of the Scots and English parliaments seem appealing. It took place in 1707. In the eighteenth century, improvements in agriculture resulted in more food being grown and general economic growth enabled people to buy it. There were still many years to come when there were acute local shortages of food – years of short corn – but in the nineteenth and twentieth centuries poor diet has been a far greater source of ill health.

2 Medical traditions

In the seventeenth century there were few people in Lowland Scotland with medical training, and many of them had learned their art abroad. In the Highlands and Islands, however, the Gaelic medical tradition was alive. It was a central part of Gaelic culture; a large proportion of the Scots Gaelic manuscripts which survive are medical. The traditions were handed down within families: just as the MacCrimmons were hereditary pipers, the Beatons and the McConachers were physicians. The McConachers came from Lorn, the Beatons, to give them their English name, the MacBeathadhs or Macbeths, were spread all over the Highlands and Islands. Their name means 'son of life'.

The Gaelic tradition, as far as we can appreciate it, was the European tradition of the late Middle Ages, based on the texts of ancient Greeks, particularly the Hippocratic collection (5th-4th century BC), ancient Romans such as Galen (129-99 BC), medieval Arabs of whom Avicenna (AD 980-1037) was the most important, Guy de Chauliac (1298?-1386) and other Continental writers. To their works, Gaelic physicians added a commentary, writing paragraphs in the margins of the manuscripts which expanded or corrected the text, often based on personal experience. It was thus a living tradition, growing and changing. We can appreciate it from manuscripts, but it must also have had an oral component. Celtic society included men who were respected for their medical learning in the seventh century, long before the full European tradition was shaped and then transmitted to Ireland and Scotland. These early medical men have left no remains, and their knowledge was passed by word of mouth from generation to generation. This probably continued after Hippocrates arrived in the Hebrides.

There was also a pragmatic side to medical treatment. In the absence of a scientific understanding of the nature of disease, 'cures' or 'remedies' were devised and tried, and they gained a reputation if they were successful. For example, a man on the Isle of Harris had found how to treat himself:

> John Campbell, Forester of *Harries* [Harris], makes use of this singular Remedy for a Cold: He walks into the Sea up to the middle with his Clothes on, and immediately after goes to bed in his wet Clothes, and then laying the Bed-clothes over him, procures a Sweat, which removes the Distemper.

Complex explanations were not sought where superficial ones seemed adequate. Practical cures which appeared to work had power at a time when so little was understood. Extreme emotions were thought to have the power to kill: the poet William Drummond of Hawthornden was believed to have expired of grief in 1649 when he heard the news of the execution of King Charles I, and it was said that twelve years later Sir Thomas Urquhart of Cromarty laughed so much at the news of the Restoration of the monarchy that he too died.

The recorder of John Campbell's cure was Martin Martin whose *Description of the Western Islands of Scotland* (1703) contains much fascinating material on the practice of medicine. He studied medicine at the University of Leiden in the Netherlands, so he was well able to make observations of medicine and health, and in South Uist he met one of the Beaton family, Fergus. Martin tells us that in Skye, where he was born, the chief diseases were 'fevers, stiches, cholick, head-ach, megrim, jaundice, sciatica, stone, small-pox, measles, rickets, scurvy, worms, fluxes [diarrhoea], tooth-ach, cough and squinance [tonsillitis]'. To us, this is as much a list of symptoms as of diseases. Martin describes the different ways in which herbs were used, as ointments and plasters as well as internally. Always he sees man as a part of nature, an animal whose health can be maintained with plants – and then he breaks off to say that seaweed can be a good manure for fruit trees.

The Gaelic tradition in medicine faded out in the middle of the eighteenth century, but contemporaries regarded its last significant representative as John Beaton, one of the Beatons of Pennycross, and Minister of Kilninian in Mull, who died in 1714. He was a transitional figure, educated at the Grammar School at Inveraray and at Glasgow University. Beaton was a man of great ability and an authority on Gaelic customs, history and genealogy, as well as medicine. His ministry came to an end following the Glorious Revolution of 1689-90: he refused to become a minister of the presbyterian church. He remained with his episcopal flock, impoverished, marginalized. But he was consulted by the ever-inquisitive Sibbald and visited by the Welsh antiquary Edward Lluyd, who valued his learning. During his lifetime we also find Gaelic medical practitioners appearing in Lowland Scotland, such as Iomhar MacNeill, 'stone cutter' – operator on bladder stones – to the city of Glasgow, and his successor in 1688, Duncan Campbell.

Gaelic physicians and surgeons did not actively seek new discoveries. Their learning became separated from the European mainstream before the discoveries in anatomy in northern Italy in the sixteenth century, which started the continuous investigations which have utterly altered medicine in the last four centuries. This new learning was based on observation, not tradition, and it was exemplified by the scrupulous examination of the body by the anatomist Andreas Vesalius (1514-64) who came from Brussels but worked in Padua, and the innovative practical surgery of the Frenchman Ambrose Paré (1510-90). Their approach was adopted by the medical men in Glasgow, Edinburgh and Aberdeen, and it was the route to increased knowledge.

The work of Paré was made known by Peter Lowe of Glasgow in his *Discourse of the Whole Art of Chirurgerie* (1597). Lowe had studied and practised on the Continent, and he returned not only with knowledge but with a desire to promote the profession by organizing it: he was the driving force behind the founding of the

Faculty of Physicians and Surgeons of Glasgow in 1599. In Edinburgh, the Incorporation of Surgeons was granted its Seal of Cause by the Town Council in 1505, and ratified the following year by King James IV – a Renaissance man who had medical training and skills. The College of Physicians followed in 1681.

Sibbald was one of the first fellows of the Royal College of Physicians; another was Archibald Pitcairne, physician, playwright, and near-atheist. He became Professor of Medicine at Leiden in the Netherlands in 1692, and when he died his library was bought by Peter the Great and shipped to St Petersburg. Like Sibbald, he was a figure of European standing. Pitcairne, a Jacobite, was accused of writing a letter critical of the government – in effect, of high treason – and he escaped by saying he was drunk at the time. He was buried with a case of wine beside him, and left a jeroboam to be opened 'at the restoration' of the Stuart monarchy. Decades later the headstone on his grave was repaired, and this was taken to be a sufficient restoration to justify broaching the bottle. Yet for all their ability, their individualism and Jacobite politics prevented Sibbald and Pitcairne from establishing a medical school in Scotland.

Medicine was still to separate itself from other activities. James Borthwick (1615-1675) was a leading surgeon and apothecary in Edinburgh. In 1674 he treated the dying Marchioness of Douglas with plasters, poultices and purges: the old woman must have suffered unnecessarily in her last days. After her death Borthwick embalmed her with 'balsames, lotiones, oyles & sweet oyles'. He was paid more for them than for his medical services. The medical institutions, by establishing monopolies and improving education, helped to create the profession of medicine, separating the physician and surgeon from the quack, the barber, the undertaker and the apothecary.

One of the gardeners talking to Professor John Hope in the Botanic Garden, Edinburgh, where medicinal plants were grown. John Kay's etching dates from 1786.

3 The Edinburgh medical school

In 1663 Alexander Alexander of Edinburgh was cautioned for 'taiking upon him to use chirurgerie and use the pairt of a doctor and apothecar unskillfully without being approvin by the chirurgians and doctors.' He was a gardener, and probably thought he could deploy his knowledge of medicinal herbs in a new career.

The reaction of the physicians and surgeons shows that they were already well-developed professions with agreed standards of competence. Their training began with apprenticeship, and might include some time in a university, probably on the Continent, perhaps at Paris or Rheims. For a surgeon, experience in war was highly valued, and the teaching of Latin in Scottish schools made it possible for surgeons to serve with foreign regiments.

By the end of the seventeenth century Sibbald and others understood that improvements in medical practice would stem from better teaching, and that it could most effectively take place in some form of institution. The scene was prepared for one of the most distinctive phases in Scottish cultural history.

The Edinburgh medical school was known throughout the world, and for a few decades in the middle and end of the eighteenth century, when Leiden was in decline and before the rise of Paris, it gave the best medical education. It was the first medical faculty in a British university, founded in 1726 as the result of some thoughtful manoeuvring by a surgeon, John Monro, and the powerful and manipulative George Drummond, the Lord Provost. They both saw the city declining because the wealth which had accompanied the meeting of the Scots parliament had been taken instead to London after the Union of the Parliaments in 1707. Their idea was that a world-class medical school would attract young men of substance from Scotland, England and abroad. In politics, both were strongly in favour of the Hanoverian succession: Monro and his son treated soldiers after the battle against Jacobites at Sheriffmuir in 1715. They were able to bring their plans to fruition.

The Scots novelist and physician Tobias Smollett described the medical school in 1771, around its peak:

> The university of Edinburgh is supplied with excellent professors in all the sciences; and the medical school, in particular, is famous all over Europe. – The students of this art have the best opportunity of learning it to perfection, in all its branches, as there are different courses for the *theory of medicine* and the *practice of medicine;* for *anatomy, chemistry, botany,* and the *materia medica,* over and above those of *mathematics* and *experimental philosophy;* and all these are given by men of distinguished talents. What renders this part of education still more complete, is the advantage of attending the infirmary, which is the best instituted charitable foundation that I ever knew.

Of the three dozen or so men who had medical chairs in Edinburgh in the eighteenth century, many were fine teachers and many made significant advances in medicine and science. At the core of the teaching was anatomy. The first professor, from 1720 until his death, was Alexander Monro *primus* (1697-1767), author of *The Anatomy of the Human Bones* (1726), and he was followed by his equally able son Alexander Monro *secundus* (1733-1817). *Tertius* (1773-1859) showed the medical school in descent from its zenith: he was wordy in print, and woolly in thought. He was little respected, and a story was invented that he read from his lecture notes the words 'when I was at Leyden in 1719', implying that they had been written by his grandfather.

The Edinburgh professors, these 'men of distinguished talents' were individuals, often jealous of one another. They were in competition with medical lecturers outside the university, men of learning and high reputation: all wanted students, for students paid fees. The aggressive James Gregory walked round the town with his cane over his shoulder, and when he met his colleague James Hamilton, the obstetrician, with whom he was engaged in a particularly stormy teacup, he beat him about the shoulders. Taken to court, Gregory was fined £100 and announced he would pay the same again for another chance.

As a scientist, one man stands out from the rest – Joseph Black (1728-99). Born of a Scots-Irish family in Bordeaux, Black was educated at Glasgow: he was Professor of Anatomy there from 1756, and of chemistry at Edinburgh from 1766. Black's first discovery was 'fixed air' – the gas we now call carbon dioxide – and shortly afterwards he developed the concepts of the latent heats at changes from solid to liquid and liquid to gas, and of specific heat. These achievements belong to chemistry and physics, not to medicine, but what is important here is that Black was extending the use of measurement in science by using the chemical balance and the thermometer. He taught his discoveries as soon as they were made to his medical students.

Another innovator was William Buchan, author of *Domestic Medicine* (1769). He said he was 'laying medicine more open to mankind', making it intelligible to ordinary people in contrast with the abstruseness of eighteenth-century pharmacopoeiae. He was closely associated with another popularizer of knowledge, William Smellie, the initiator of the *Encyclopedia Britannica*. Buchan wrote of cures, but also of preventing illness and maintaining health by exercise and a sound diet.

One professor, Andrew Duncan (1744-1828), was responsible for several important developments. He set up a long-running medical journal. Following the death in 1774 of the poet Robert Fergusson in the Edinburgh Bedlam (which was in Bristo, just west of the present National Museums' site in Edinburgh) he campaigned for humane treatment of the mentally ill, and the Royal Edinburgh Asylum for the Insane was finally founded in 1807. He promoted discussion among students through the Royal Medical Society, which awarded him a gold medal in 1787 in recognition of his work. Duncan set up the Edinburgh Public Dispensary (1776) to give cheap medical services to those who could not afford full professional fees. He was a cheerful and sociable man who organized dining clubs and social activities for his fellow medics. In an era when many students remained poor until long after qualifying, he paid for the burials of those who

Chemical balance used by Professor Joseph Black, 1760-1790. This is possibly the instrument which he used in making his discoveries, but it is more likely to have been for lecturing.

Black lecturing, as seen by John Kay (1787).

died young, and their little headstones surround his own in Buccleuch burying ground.

The need to understand the body by studying anatomy was fully understood by 1800: verbal descriptions in lectures were insufficient. The reality of dissection was essential. The medical students looked on the corpses they dissected with affection: the dead were helping them to become professionals. The 'subject' was known as the *shusy*, a variant of the name Susie. But medical education was booming, and there were not enough *shusies*.

The Anatomy Act (1832) ensured a supply of suitable corpses by making available the unclaimed bodies of paupers. Before that, though, there were acute difficulties, for the supply for subjects for dissection could only be maintained by robbing fresh graves before the bodies had begun to decompose. Authority tended to turn a blind eye when it could, but popular feeling was violently against the anatomists. Relatives would stand guard over a burial, and some parishes built watch houses for them. In other places headstones were replaced by horizontal stone slabs, or by cast iron defences – mortsafes. The National Museums have one from Airth in Stirlingshire which was made in 1831 and which fitted over the coffin like a larger, bottomless coffin. It weighs 400 kilograms.

This brings us to the unpleasant figures of William Burke and William Hare, suppliers of subjects to the medical schools of Edinburgh. When in 1827 they ran short of bodies to sell to the brilliant Dr Robert Knox, they turned to murder – for which Burke was hung after Hare turned King's Evidence. The mob chanted:

> Up the close and doon the stair
> Ben the hoose wi Burke an Hare
> Burke's the bully, Hare's the thief
> And Knox the boy who buys the beef.

Burke's body was dissected in public by Monro *tertius*.

Though the store of available knowledge was increasing, the developments affected only the few patients who had access to a doctor – the rich and their households, and the city dwellers who

The Kingskettle (Fife) collar, about 1825. It held a buried corpse so that 'resurrectionists' could not remove it for anatomical dissection.

ELEGY

Part of a hand-bill printed immediately after - and probably written before - Burke's execution in 1829. His corpse was 'anatomised'.

ON
WILLIAM BURKE,

Who was Executed at Edinburgh, Jan. 28, 1829.

EPITAPH.

New Burke's away, his life's extinct,
  And past a' men's protection,
He's made a subject new himsel',
  His body's for dissection.
Poor Willie, if his soul be weel,
  It's mair than what's expecit,
For by his deeds, (if we may judge),
  By him it was neglecit.
But some fo'k thinks it has nae chance,
  In Heaven for to dwell,
If that's the case, there's ae thing sure,
  It is consign'd to H–ll !

BY A COUNTRYMAN

could find a medical man who was prepared to treat them at little or no cost, or who could gain admission to a hospital. There were very few hospitals.

Consequently traditional or folk medicine was still central to the lives of nine-tenths of Scots. Though the educated medic preferred to see a gulf between his own rational medicine and the superstitious practices of tradition, there were many points of contact between the two. The minister of West Linton in Peeblesshire reported that about 1765:

> A man called William Badie, or Beattie, a shoe-maker, being afflicted with stomach complaints, contracted by drinking cold water when overheated in harvest, he was advised to swallow stones to help digestion, after the manner of birds with muscular stomachs. He was ever after afflicted with violent stomach complaints, and frequent vomitings, with a long train of nervous symptoms. He never suspected that the stones had lodged in his stomach, till happening to be seised with a vomiting, lying across a bed, with his head and body reclined downwards ... He threw up 13, which being the Devil's dozen, might probably be the number swallowed.

If there is a superstitious element in this, there was also an irrational aspect to one of the most important parts of scientific medicine: the appointment of professors of medicine. Edinburgh University had been founded by the Town Council in 1582. In the middle of the nineteenth century the Council still chose many of the professors. James Syme, professor of surgery, explained in 1855:

> Every candidate ... must personally canvass all of those individuals and bring influence to bear upon each of them. He must publish volumes of testimonials, and have a committee constantly in action to promote his claims ... The patrons ... have no means of knowing the merits of the candidates, except through testimonials, as to the respective value of which they are incompetent to judge.

It was not a system which guaranteed the best result. One councillor in 1855 favoured a particular candidate because he had written with affection of his mother: this was supposed to show sound professional attitudes. Syme was arguing for the autonomy of the medical profession, and for decisions of medical ability to be made by medical men.

Edinburgh University was removed from Council control in 1858 and the filling of chairs then bore more relation to professional judgements of candidates' knowledge and experience. In the same year Parliament passed the Medical Act which required that all practitioners in the future should have recognized qualifications and that the name of every doctor should be printed in the annual *Medical Register*. It was the end of the old system of training by apprenticeship, and was a step in the marginalization of the quack.

4 Wells and the power of water

The practice of visiting wells, and of drinking or bathing at them, was central to beliefs about health and the curing of illness from the Middle Ages to the eighteenth century, and in many places until the middle of the nineteenth century. There were wells all over Scotland, some more famous than others, some with an international renown and great powers. 'The well of Kildinguie will cure all ills except the Black Death': this was a well on the island of Stronsay in the Orkneys, and it was known in Norway. Many wells were springs, but others were holes in rocks where water collected. These might be beside a river, as St Walloch's Well on the upper reaches of the Deveron, on the edge of the Grampian Mountains, or the Well of the Co', in a cove on the seashore near the Mull of Galloway. Some wells produced water which might be carried miles to the sick bed; at the same time every well or stream on which *biolair* [water cress] grew was health-giving.

Before the arrival of Christianity, wells were seen as bringers of health – and perhaps even life itself – from the heart of the Earth. They had great significance, and when the new religion arrived priests did not discourage people from using healing wells. Instead they dedicated them to Christian saints and drew them into religious practice. On the island of Eigg in the Inner Hebrides Martin Martin recorded in 1703 that:

> there is a Well, call'd St. Katherine's Well, the Natives have it in great Esteem, and believe it to be a Catholicon [universal cure] for Diseases. They told me it had been such every since it had been consecrated by one Father Hugh, in the following manner: He oblig'd all the Inhabitants to come to this Well, and then imploy'd them to bring together a great heap of Stones at the Head of the Spring, by way of Penance. This being done, he said Mass at the Well, and then consecrated it; he gave each of the Inhabitants a piece of Wax Candle, which they lighted, and all of them made the Dessil, [that is] of going round the well Sunways, the Priest leading them.

It was usual to leave a gift, a pin or a coin, at a well, or to tie a strip of rag round a nearby bush or tree. The latter practice is still carried on at St Mary's Well at Culloden, east of Inverness, and at wells on the Black Isle – one of them significantly known as the *Clootie Well*. The idea is that the piece of cloth holds the troubles of the person who leaves it, and that they can be left at the well. In Ancient Rome it was common to give thanks for a cure by presenting to the temple a model of the once-diseased part, and the leaving of this kind of votive offering became part of medieval religious observance. It remained at some wells in Scotland, such as St Thenew's in Glasgow. A tinsmith is said to have found full-time employment making arms, legs, noses and so on for pilgrims whose illness had been removed by the saint or her well. St Thenew or Enoch was the mother of St Mungo, the patron of Glasgow, and her chapel and well were removed when St Enoch's station was built. A shopping centre now stands on the site.

Some wells had a guardian in the form of an animal. Most often this was a fish or a worm; at St Michael's Well in Strath Avon in Banffshire there was a more unusual presence, as the minister explained in 1794:

> the winged guardian, under the semblance of a fly, was never absent from his duty. If the sober matron wished to know of her

husband's ailment, or the love-sick nymph that of her languishing swain, they visited the well. Every movement of the sympathetic fly was regarded in silent awe; and as he appeared cheerful or dejected, the anxious votaries drew their presages. Like the King of Great Britain, whom a fiction of the English law supposes never to die, the guardian fly of the Well of St Michael, was believed to be exempted from the laws of mortality.

A quartz crystal used as a medical charm. It was dipped in water and the water drunk by the sufferer.

The power of healing wells was thought to be greatest at the beginning of each quarter of the Celtic year, on the first Sunday after All Hallows Day, Candlemas, Beltane and Lammas. The two last – 1 May and 1 August – were more important because it was easier to make a pilgrimage in summer. Wells were used by all classes. At the most celebrated wells large crowds gathered, as much for meeting and merrymaking as for devotion and health. Up to the end of the eighteenth century the whole parish would go to the Well of the Co' at Beltane, and bathe and sit on the rocks and enjoy the beginning of summer. Grew's Well at Dunkeld was particularly popular on the first Sunday in May, and there were many booths there selling drink. This was a powerful well, visited at the beginning of July for whooping-cough and at any time for rheumatism and the stone (bladder stones).

The Reformation brought a complete change in the church's attitude to wells. The visiting of wells was condemned by Kirk Sessions as a superstitious ritual, and from their minute books we can learn which wells were popular in the sixteenth and seventeenth centuries. Just south of Aberdeen is St Fittack's Well which was used for curing the sick when in 1636 'Margrat Davidson was adjudget to an outlaw of five pounds for directing her nurs with her bairne to St Fithack's well, and washine the bairn thairin for the recovery of her health and for leaveing an offering at the well.' St Queran's Well is on the flat ground south-west of Dumfries, and in 1642 Dorothy Harries and Marion Hairson were censured for going there 'on the first Sunday in May in ane superstitious way to fetch the waters thereof [and] are ordained to acknowledge their offence in the body of the church on Sunday.' In Aberdeenshire the Well of the Virgin Mary at Chapel of Seggat was widely known – it was visited by King James IV in 1504 – and the kirk twice had it filled with stones, but it was emptied by local people and survives. Robert Burns visited the Brow Well on the shores of the Solway the week before he died. It still bubbles today, albeit in a brick-lined trough.

Beside a well, the *tobar na bile*, near the south end of Loch Awe in Argyllshire, is a small graveyard. There was found a slip of elephant ivory some 185 mm long, known as Barbreck's bone. It has been cut to a rectangular shape: probably it was once mounted on a medieval reliquary, and was lost or hidden in the graveyard. After its rediscovery it was regarded as a charm against madness. Part of its significance was its oddness, but it was also special because of the location in which it had been found.

Rational medicine also believed in the curative power of water, and as transport became easier, mineral wells became popular places to seek health. Their benefits came not from the purity of the water, but from the salts it contained: just as wells were traditionally believed to have their own identities, now the mineral content of each well was measured by chemists and their possible effects published. Some doctors were sceptical about the power of well water: Joseph Black saw the crowd visiting St Bernard's Well by the Water of Leith, and said that the benefit of going there came from the exercise during the walk.

Some villages discovered a new prosperity from valetudinarians: Moffat erected a handsome monument to John Williamson who had discovered a chalybeate well on the side of Hartfell in 1748. The most wealthy might travel to Karlsbad in Bohemia: a description of its waters was published in the *Scots Magazine* in 1757; others went to Strathpeffer or Bridge of Earn. Yet the power of water over the darker forces was still well-known; running water saved the life of Tam o' Shanter after he disturbed the hellish legion.

5 Medical life

Oh, a pleasant thing, surely, it is to get Fees,
When so many hard struggles we have with Disease.

In the eighteenth and nineteenth centuries doctors received their income in the form of fees from their patients. Most were able to make themselves quietly comfortable and in the little world of the parish place themselves almost on the same social level as the minister. Part of their income came from the drugs they sold, for most acted as apothecaries as well as doctors. Thus the incompetent John Hornbook in Burns' poem 'Death and Dr Hornbook':

A' the doctor's saws and whittles,
Of a' dimensions, shapes an' mettles,
A' kinds o' boxes, mugs and bottles,
He's sure to hae;
Their Latin names as fast he rattles
As ABC.

In the larger towns a socially dexterous man could, with some ability in medicine, make himself wealthy, though not as rich as the leading physicians and surgeons in London.

The difficulty was to get started, to find the first patients who would recommend the young doctor to their friends. Testimonials helped. James Gregory (1753-1821), Professor of the Practice of Medicine at Edinburgh, described his pupil John Thomson in 1810 as being

of good temper, and of great prudence, of excellent talents, a complete classical scholar, (as to Greek and Latin,) and thoroughly well instructed in all the various branches of medical science.

TO THE MOST BOUNTEOUS PUBLIC.

JUST arrived from his Travels, that celebrated Preserver of Men's Constitutions, Doctor VON MORDICAI MUNDUNGUS; who, without any vanity for his own unequalled abilities, Cures, in a shorter time than was ever before attempted, every Disease that is, and is not, mentioned in the list, being determined to Kill or Cure. Dead Men restored in the newest fashion, by swallowing only two quarts of Elixir Vitæ. The following list shews the Complaints relieved both in Men, Women, and Beasts, by his sovereign Specific,

Bunyons,   Burns,
Bald Heads.

Brains put in Order by the Day, Month or Year.

Broken Heads	Cholics
Broken Tails	Coughs
Broken Shins	Cold
Broken Legs	Catarrhs
Broken Arms	Corns
Broken Wind	Cuts :

Cosmetics for the Fair Sex;

Who are also supplied with Teeth, Eyes of any Hue, Patches; and, in short, every Feature, repaired amazingly cheap, and on the shortest notice.—N. B. Noses, with or without Spectacles; Old Ladies privately supplied with the Doctor's unrivalled Anticholicus, or Venterotiate, for the dispersing or raising the *Wind*.

This most celebrated Physician has the honor of acquainting the Public, how superior a method he has of cutting Corns and Toe-nails with a Saw: He Bleeds also with a two-pronged Fork when no Lancet is at hand, and dry-shaves Heads with an Iron Hoop, so as not to discompose the Patient.

N. B. Ladies and Gentlemen killed on the shortest notice, with or without pain, and at a reduced price.—Servants and Children extra.

The Doctor may be consulted at his House, No. 1. Puffmaker Row, Edinburgh, from 4 to 8.

The order in which Gregory listed Thomson's virtues is significant: his character first, his knowledge of ancient languages next, and finally the practical matter of medicine.

The young medical man was aware that luck might bring him fame. One day about 1780 James Dempster, a well-known Edinburgh jeweller, when very drunk threatened to cut his own throat. One of his companions, equally intoxicated, said, 'I will save you the trouble', and advanced with a knife. He stumbled, and accidentally wounded Dempster. John Bennett, a young surgeon, arrived quickly and closed and dressed the cut. The story went round the town, and Bennett became a public figure after a few minutes' work.

The life of the country doctor was different. John Goodsir of Largo (born 1746), was educated at Edinburgh University, but he preferred life in the Fife countryside to the intensely competitive world of city medicine. He spent most of his week on horseback. 'Dr Goodsir would start from Largo on Monday caparisoned for the week with drugs and surgical appliances ... To obviate the dangers of travelling by night, he carried a lantern, fastened to a strap above his knee.' The people of Fife were fortunate in living in a wealthy county close to the capital. John Galt's novel of Ayrshire life, *Annals of the Parish* (1821), describes towns and villages in which there were no medical practitioners. In the course of his narrative doctors arrive, some looking for work, some brought by groups of weavers. In the eighteenth century the lack of country doctors meant that local people of some education had to fill the gap. When smallpox was a great killer some ministers used the pulpit to recommend inoculation, and themselves inoculated children on a Sunday morning, before or after the service.

It was one thing to build up a practice: the doctor then had to collect his fees. At Creetown, on the Wigtownshire coast, early in

Medical lampoon, about 1830, satirizing the way in which doctors boasted of their skill in a highly competitive environment.

the nineteenth century, the local doctor complained that

> half o' the natives was Eerish, an gied him neathing but thanks, an'
> the lave o' them was gentilities yt keepit him rinnin' efter them
> nicht an' day, an' gied him naething but an ill name when he
> crave't them for siller.

During the eighteenth century, hospitals were founded in the larger burghs. The first was the Royal Infirmary in Edinburgh (1729). Others followed, including those in Aberdeen (1742), Dumfries (1776) and Dundee (1798). They raised money from charitable donations, subscriptions which allowed the donor to recommend patients worthy of treatment, and church collections. Dundee Infirmary received fines imposed by the courts, as in 1822-3, 'A fine awarded for a gentleman riding through a field of new grass – 21 shillings; for butter seized in public market, being under weight – 31 shillings.' These hospitals were for apparently curable patients; provision for incurables did not take place until the nineteenth century.

Georgian hospitals were economic buildings much like other buildings on the same scale, whether homes or warehouses. High Victorian hospital architecture emphasized height and bulk: to stand close to the Royal Infirmary, Edinburgh, was to be dominated by its size. The high ceilings were needed for good ventilation, and the effect on poor people who lived in cramped tenement flats with low ceilings must have been extraordinary. The hospital was a palace where air and light travelled everywhere – but so did the eye of the representative of medical authority, the nurse. Only the disciplined would be cured.

Hospitals in the country were often mental hospitals, and were more strange. The Scotch baronial style, tall and turreted, was common. The hospital was a species of country house; even if it was bare inside, the families who had left patients there could feel that the guilt of desertion was limited by the grandiose surroundings. Often there was more than one building, as at Sunnyside near Montrose, where one house was for so-called paupers, the other for those who could pay. The latter had more space and amenities, including a small theatre. Many of the country hospitals projected a gothic horror from their looming bulk and steep-pitched roofs and towers – towers which might appear an architectural extravagance, but usually contained the main water tank. Among mature trees above the River Cart between Glasgow and Paisley stands Leverndale, a refuge for the sick in mind: in mist, or at twilight, its jagged skyline projects unspeakable threats. Yet, at the same time, the asylum was a place of

Montrose Lunatic Asylum, opened in 1784, on a Montrose trade token of 1796.

safe retreat, the large buildings reassuring in their solidity, the parkland calm. The Crichton Royal Hospital at Dumfries is a fine example.

6 The cholera and other infections

At the beginning of the nineteenth century many diseases were still regarded as the product of the environment. For example, scurvy afflicted most of the ordinary people in Orkney in the 1770s. They thought that it was caused by damp in the sea air, and the cold of winter. The usual cure was to take flowers of brimstone – sulphur – or to rub the skin with it. The sulphur felt hot, and so was supposed to drive away the disease. In the same decade James Lind realised that a diet containing fresh vegetables or lime juice would prevent scurvy, but it was not for another 150 years that it was understood to be a deficiency disease, caused by lack of vitamin C.

The climate and the fluctuations of the weather were understood to have a large influence on health. This lies behind the comments of an Englishman on the establishing of a garrison at

Fort Augustus, at the south end of Loch Ness: 'if the inhabitants of the new settlement proposed, could have lived upon Air, I verily believe they would have been fed with better diet than at Montpellier.' The freshness of the air, its dampness or dryness, and the nature of the winds were all important.

These ideas about the benefits of a healthy environment form the background to the cholera epidemic which hit Scotland in 1832. It had begun several years earlier in the Punjab, and swept inexorably westwards. From the Baltic it was brought by ship to Sunderland, and it soon spread over the rest of the British Isles. Dumfries suffered especially badly. It is commemorated by a monument in St Michael's churchyard, where 350 of the victims were buried under a single mound, and by a vivid passage in William McDowall's *History of the Burgh of Dumfries* (1867):

> The scavenging [refuse collection] was deficient; the drainage merely nominal; and, worse of all, the water supply was limited and impure. With the exception of what was furnished by a few wells and private pumps, all the water used for domestic purposes was carried by hand or carter in barrels from the Nith by four old men, who doled it out in tin pitchers or cans, from door to door, at the rate of five canfuls a penny. The river, when swelled by heavy rains, which was often the case, became thick with mud; and it was constantly exposed to a more vexatious pollution, caused by the refuse poured into it from the town. The quality of the water did not improve by being borne about in barrels of suspicious aspect; and often, indeed, the liquid drawn from them during summer acquired a taste-me-not repulsiveness by the presence of innumerable little objects, pleasant to no one save an enthusiast in entomology.

When the burgh had grown in the Middle Ages, the houses were built close together so that the town might be more easily defended, 'and when the cholera came, these places of defence were its chief objects of attack.' The progress of the disease was watched as it approached from one hamlet to another, and it arrived in the burgh in the middle of September. In the first week there was only one death a day, and the people thought that it was a modified, less virulent form of the disease. Alas, Dumfries was mistaken. The disease spread swiftly until 44 died on 2 October. The situation was terrifying, but equally suddenly, equally inexplicably, the epidemic abated and the temporary cholera hospital closed on 13 November. In just over a month 550 had died in a population of 10,000.

The cholera was believed to be both infectious and contagious. 'It was supposed that an affected individual distilled a poisonous influence all around him; that there was death in his touch; and that the virus of the malady lurked in every article of his dress.' In this traditional view, it was almost impossible to

The monument in St Michael's churchyard, Dumfries, to the cholera victims of 1832. Robert Burns is buried nearby.

IN THIS CEMETERY,
and chiefly within this enclosure,
lie the mortal remains
of more than 420 inhabitants of Dumfries,
who were suddenly swept away
by the memorable invasion of
Asiatic Cholera
A.D. MDCCCXXXII.
That terrific Pestilence
entered the Town on 15th September,
and remained till 27th November,
during which period it seized
at least 900 individuals,
of whom 44 died in one day
and no more than 415 were reported
as recovered:
That the benefit of this
solemn warning
might not be lost to posterity
this monument
was erected from collections made in
several Churches in this Town.

prevent the disease or to treat sufferers. Medical opinion, how-ever, was beginning to see the vital importance of clean water and good sanitation. After another cholera outbreak in 1848-9, a Bill was presented to parliament for the engineering of a new water supply for Dumfries: when the news arrived that the Preamble was proved – that Parliament was going to pass the Act – the bells were rung and bonfires lit. Water started to flow in 1851. Other places had poor water supply. Edinburgh, unusually for a major city, is not on a river, and it was perennially short of water until by 1890 it was served by 13 reservoirs. Dundee too had a poor water supply: in 1861 it had a population of 91,000 and only five water closets. Three of them were in hotels. The main well was the Ladywell, whose name shows that before the Reformation it had been dedicated to the Virgin Mary. Once valued for the purity of its water it was unfortunately next to the slaughterhouse, and helped to spread smallpox, cholera, typhus, and typhoid.

Smallpox had been a major killer in the eighteenth century: 'The smashing that it made of the poor bits o' bairns was indeed woeful.' At the end of the century it caused nineteen per cent of all deaths, and thirty per cent of deaths under the age of five. Vaccination with a mild form of the disease, cow pox, was becom-ing recognized as the method of preventing smallpox, but it was still regarded with suspicion: from time to time there were fatal-ities. However, the reason why inoculation worked was not understood. Smallpox had almost been eradicated from Western Europe by 1950 and the last case in the world occurred in 1978.

The nineteenth century was a period of rapid growth in medical knowledge. The physiology of the body and the nature of many diseases became better understood through the use of the microscope. Germans were at the forefront of the development of bacteriology when in the last two decades of the nineteenth century it began to explain the causes of specific diseases. The diphtheria bacillus was discovered in Zürich in 1883, that of tetanus in Berlin in 1889, of bubonic plague in Hong Kong in 1894. The individual who made the largest contribution was

Robert Koch (1843-1910), who discovered the bacilli of tuberculosis in 1882 and cholera in 1883. Yet the fact that a microbe could be identified and given a name did not mean that the fight was over.

Two Scots made contributions to this story. Rudolph Virchow, one of the greatest of nineteenth-century biologists, dedicated his great book on cellular pathology to John Goodsir (1814-67), whose grandfather we have already met, riding through Fife in the dark. Goodsir was born in Fife, at Anstruther, and was educated both at St Andrews and Edinburgh. In the mid 1830s he was one of the first to use the microscope in anatomy, and later studied the structure and function of cells. Another Edinburgh figure, John Hughes Bennett (1812-75) was a pioneer of microscopic pathology and in 1845 the first to describe a blood disease: he named it leucocythemia, and today we call in leukaemia.

7 The Medical Officer of Health

It is one thing to be in the laboratory and see the bacillus which causes a disease; it is another to act on the scale which will eradicate that disease.

By 1800, Glasgow was Scotland's second largest city; by 1914 it was the second city of the British Empire. Its industrial base was shipbuilding and every kind of engineering. It was a commercial centre, and the banks of the Clyde were lined with wharves. It grew with tremendous speed, faster than houses could be built, and the city's success depended on cheap labour, on men, women and children crammed into hovels. After an epidemic of relapsing fever in 1843 one doctor observed that the houses at the bottom of the Molendinar valley beneath Glasgow Cathedral were not fit for pigs; and another went into dwellings east of the Saltmarket and found pigs and donkeys sleeping in the same rooms as people. In 1871, 41% of Glasgow families lived in a single room. These slums were ravaged by infectious diseases, particularly typhus.

Mother and child in a Glasgow slum, about 1900.

Glasgow was fortunate that during this period its Medical Officer of Health was James Russell (1837-1904), Glasgow-born, Glasgow-trained and completely committed to the reduction of disease and the improvement of the health of the citizens. Russell wrote the clearest prose – a vital skill because part of this job was to submit reports to the Town Council, laymen who had to understand what he had found, be shocked by it, and take action. Long before the televised investigative documentary Russell shaped public opinion by lectures and pamphlets: he told the people to agitate, to put pressure on the Corporation, and the Corporation paid him to do it. He wrote:

> There are certain conditions of health for the provision and main-
> tenance of which the authorities are responsible. These are – clean
> soil upon which to stand; pure water and pure air, with all the

subsidiary arrangements for drainage, cleansing, and scavenging [refuse collection]. It is especially necessary in the interest of the small householder that the authorities should do their duty in these regards. Even he is a ratepayer, and can make his voice heard through his representatives.

The filth and stench of an early Victorian city are incomprehensible to us today. Part of the difficulty lay in the ownership of the slums by private landlords who would gain nothing from improvements in sanitation. In any case, radical demolition in one area would only have increased the overcrowding elsewhere. Where Glasgow Corporation could act, it did. It proposed a huge water supply scheme, and when it was rejected by parliament the city employed the most famous engineers of the day, the two great railway pioneers, Isambard Kingdom Brunel and Robert

Water supply in Biggar, Lanarkshire, about 1900. Although these men are probably going to water the dusty streets, the same method had earlier been used for domestic delivery. SLA

Stephenson, to write a report endorsing the idea. The result was the Loch Katrine supply which could bring every day 50,000 gallons of pure water from the Trossachs 34 miles away, to Glasgow. It opened in 1859.

The Corporation encouraged cleanliness in other ways. The first washhouse was opened in 1878, making it possible for women to wash clothes and linen, and the buildings included baths and a swimming pool. It was at the head of Glasgow Green and on the edge of some of the worst slums – the Calton. By 1914, the city had 20 such establishments.

Russell worked with various specialists, such as the Factory Inspector. His was a vital role for many jobs were associated with particular diseases. Jute and flax workers laboured in dusty conditions, ironworkers in great heat. Lead was poisonous. Miners were at risk from flood, the fall of the roof of the seam, and gas and dust explosions – and in time the coal dust coated the fine structure of their lungs and made them unable to breathe. This disease, pneumoconiosis, also affected quarrymen.

Food was another concern of the Medical Officer of Health. As the decades passed it became clear that food which looked and smelled fresh might contain the bacteria of disease. There was more ignorance and misunderstanding in the provision trade than there was dishonesty, as Russell explained:

The physiologist and the pathologist say: 'Show us the animal when it is alive and its whole organs and parts when it has been slaughtered, and we will pronounce judgement on the wholesomeness of the whole animal.' The butcher says: 'Allow me to kill the animal and "dress" the carcase, and then I shall draw aside the curtain and admit you to the contemplation of a work of art.' So artificial is the butcher's conception of the structure and constitution of a carcase that he will confidently submit it in detachments – tongues and sirloins, rumps and quarters, chops and steaks, just

St Luke, the patron of physicians, painted about 1614 for Dean House, near Edinburgh, the home of William Nisbet of Dean.

The plague mound at
Fortingall in Glen Lyon,
Perthshire, probably a
relic of the Black Death
of 1349-50.

St Boniface's Well near
Munlochy on the Black
Isle. The sick person
leaves his or her illness in
the form of a rag or piece
of clothing: as it rots, the
illness disappears.

The temple at St Bernard's Well by the Water of Leith, 1788. Joseph Black acidly said that visitors to the well would benefit more from the walk there than from the water they drank.

The flag day was an important way of raising funds for hospitals before the advent of the National Health Service. These flags date from the 1930s.

*Henry Littlejohn
(1826-1914),
Edinburgh's Medical
Officer of Health
from 1862 to 1906, a
period when public
health measures and
improved diet
reduced the death
rate.*

*Professor John
Mallard of Aberdeen
with the 'mouse box'
(1974), which pro-
duced an image of the
body of a mouse – a
step towards Magnetic
Resonance Imaging.*

as a man might submit fossils to the geologist, taking to himself credit all the while for frankness to the Inspector, and fair play to the consumer.

Measuring the quality of milk in the laboratory at Kirkcudbright creamery in the 1950s. SLA

Russell was realistic: he recognized that butchers were mostly tradesmen of limited means, trying to make a modest living, and that in the absence of formal training it was difficult for them to understand how an apparently healthy piece of meat could be a threat to life. Thus meat inspectors were needed, men with the minds of detectives. One on Russell's staff, called Warnock, found two pieces of beef infected with tuberculosis in a van in George Square in Glasgow. They had been sent by a butcher in Moray. Warnock travelled to see him because he wanted to find the rest of the carcass:

> I found the butcher in his shop, but he declined to answer questions. A telegram from Glasgow had preceded me. After a little conversation he let fall the name of another butcher to whom he had given the missing half. When he saw I was going to visit this butcher, he said he gave away part for pigs' meat. I went to his piggery, in which were two newly-weaned pigs, and in a sleeping compartment under some straw found a fore-quarter of beef.

This missing quarter was in the other man's piggery. The butcher had sent the meat to Glasgow not by the usual railway route via Aberdeen, where dead meat was regularly inspected, but by Aviemore: he knew the meat was diseased, but did not believe it was harmful. Public health could not move forward without better public understanding.

8 The surgical revolution

Alexander Wood (1725-1807), otherwise 'Lang Sandy', was a well-known Edinburgh surgeon, loved for his kindness and respected for his skill. He was eccentric, visiting patients accompanied by his pet raven and sheep – and his humour. He took a constitutional walk to Restalrig in the evenings, and often met a tailor carrying a bundle, whom he invariably saluted with 'Weel, Tam, are ye gaun hame wi' your wark?' The tailor resented this monotonous enquiry, and one day he had his revenge. Noticing the tall figure of the well-known surgeon at the end of a funeral procession, he called 'Weel, doctor, are ye gaun hame wi' your wark?' This was not the way in which a late Victorian surgeon would have been addressed, for by 1900 he had established himself at the head of the medical world, a man with power over life and death.

There are four turning points in the history of medicine which stand out beyond all the others: the development in the middle of the sixteenth century of a new approach to anatomy based on observation; the creation of modern surgery depending on anaesthesia and the prevention of infection entering the surgical wound; the discovery of antibiotics; and the emergence in the late twentieth century of a medicine which is in constant change and which depends heavily on advanced technology. It is time to look at the second of these: it was a change in which many of the important steps took place in Scotland.

The need to operate quickly because of the patient's agony – many had died of shock – was removed in the 1840s by the discovery of effective anaesthetics. The first gas to be used was ether, but many patients found it unpleasant. In Edinburgh, a chemist suggested to James Young Simpson (1811-70) that a recently-discovered and little-known substance called chloroform might be an anaesthetic. Simpson risked trying it on himself and some friends after dinner. When they woke up under the table, they knew it worked. A few words cut into the front of his house at 52

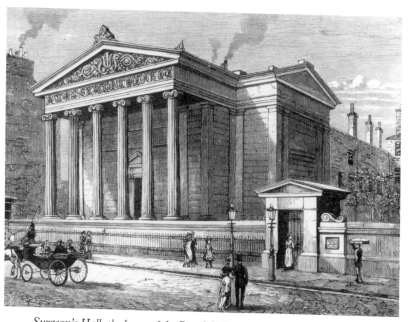

Surgeon's Hall, the home of the Royal College of Surgeons of Edinburgh, built in 1832. SLA

Queen Street commemorate the site of an important medical discovery.

Simpson was a larger than life character. Born in Bathgate, son of a baker, he was one of the medical students from poor families who had to live on the edge of starvation until they were qualified. Simpson's interest in anaesthesia was driven by his wish to ease the pains of childbirth. He found himself attacked on religious grounds. Did not the Book of Genesis say '*In sorrow* thou shalt bring forth children'? Was child bearing not intended by God to be agony? Simpson was a man of the widest reading, later President of the Society of Antiquaries of Scotland, and he was brought up in a pious Calvinist family. He took the problem seriously, and concluded that the Hebrew word which had been

Joseph Lister (1827-1912) in the middle of a group of Edinburgh medical men.

translated as *sorrow* referred to the muscular effort and struggle of birth, which still occurred under anaesthesia even though the mother was not so aware of them.

Before we approach Lister, the most famous figure, we must see the stage that surgery had reached at the time Lister reached Glasgow. One of the leading men in the profession had been Robert Liston (1794-1847), born at Ecclesmachan Manse in West Lothian, Edinburgh trained, working in London. Liston was a surgeon of the very highest skill, knowledgeable, decisive, and dexterous. He could amputate a thigh with only one assistant, compressing the artery with his left hand whilst sawing and cutting with his right. His speed in the operating theatre was legendary. Yet he was a performer rather than a thinker, and he stood for the old way of doing things. For all his success with the knife, he did not ponder on the dreadfully low survival rate of patients in the weeks after surgery. Infection easily entered the wound made as part of the operation, and there was no understanding of how to control it. The surgeon was wont to operate in an old, blood-encrusted coat.

Joseph Lister (1827-1912) was a Londoner. He had been present at the first operation performed under general anaesthesia in Britain: Liston was the surgeon. Lister moved to Edinburgh, married the daughter of the Professor of Surgery, and was appointed surgeon to Glasgow Royal Infirmary in 1860. Anaesthesia had increased the quantity of surgery being carried out, but the survival rate was still dismally low. He realized that the infection came from microorganisms in the air, and set about killing them by applying to the wound dressings soaked in carbolic acid.

Lister's steam spray being used at Aberdeen Royal Infirmary, 1889. SLA

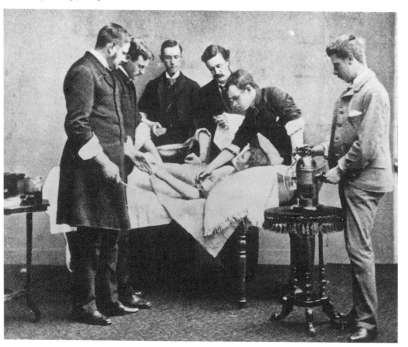

Lister extended his method in 1870 by introducing a spray which covered the wound and the area round it with a vapour of carbolic acid drops. Initially the spray was pumped by hand but by 1875 it was steam-driven: the power source behind the Industrial Revolution had reached the operating theatre. In Britain, Lister's methods were accepted with hesitation, but they caused great interest in Germany. His real achievement was in showing that the surgeon should be concerned about bacteria entering the wound.

William Macewan (1848-1924) of Glasgow, and others in Germany, developed *aseptic* rather than *antiseptic* surgery: where Lister had sought to kill bacteria, Macewen eliminated them from the surgical operation. He was not alone in arguing for this change, but he was the first. Aseptic surgery involved the sterilization by boiling of instruments and bandages, and the rigorous 'scrubbing up' by the doctors and nurses taking part in an operation. It required that surgical instruments be made in a new way, not with handles of wood or vulcanized rubber which harboured bacteria, but of a single piece of steel. This change took place quickly, between 1895 and 1900.

When Keir Hardie, the socialist leader, had his appendix removed in 1903, the operation was seen as exotic and expensive. It was paid for by public subscription, and it was looked on as a step towards a more egalitarian society, for the King himself had undergone the same operation the previous year. Yet the power and drama of surgery was not balanced by progress in other areas of medicine. Illnesses we now regard as common might not be diagnosed. Hardie suffered a series of strokes in 1907-14: they were diagnosed as temporary paralysis due to overwork. The worst one paralysed his arm, and his doctor said he had been writing too much and 'strained' the arm. He was sent to Wemyss Bay to rest.

The practice of surgery developed rapidly. It became safer to open the body cavity, to operate on all the organs and structures inside it. Macewan himself was probably the first to remove a

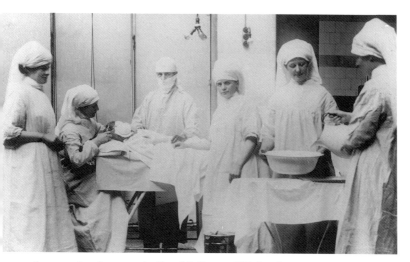

An operating theatre at the Royal Infirmary Edinburgh, about 1910. This is the aseptic era: everything possible is done to exclude germs.

lung and was certainly a pioneer of brain surgery. The senior surgeon became a figure of power, of high status, and surgeons were aware of this. Macewan was described as 'supreme and unchallenged, solitary, masterful, arrogant, intolerant and indeed selfish, but a magnificent surgeon and in his generation unique in his contribution to medical science'.

Before this period, the physician had stood at the head of the medical profession; now he was joined and perhaps overtaken by the surgeon. Hidden in laboratories, away from the sight of the public, was the third figure of power, and perhaps the most frightening of the three – the researcher. The man who discovered the bacteria which caused disease did immense good. But what if an investigator discovered an organism which could do great harm – as in one of H G Wells' short stories? What if he approached the nature of life itself? This was the question asked by Robert Louis Stevenson in *The Strange Case of Dr Jekyll and*

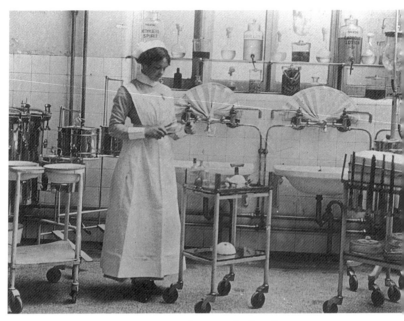

A nurse preparing an operating theatre at the Royal Infirmary, Edinburgh, 1914.

Mr Hyde (1886). The wholly evil Hyde expressed the possibilities:

> a new province of knowledge and new awareness to fame and power shall be laid open to you ... and your sight shall be blasted by a prodigy to stagger the unbelief of Satan.

And, he might have added, there were no controls to limit the behaviour of the unwise and over-ambitious seeker after fame and power. In 1997 the first successful cloning of a mammal – a sheep – was performed at Roslin near Edinburgh. This is an achievement which parallels that of Jekyll, but it was done within published guidelines and with the ethical issues beginning to be discussed in public.

9 A variety of cures

At the time when scientific medicine was advancing rapidly folk medicine was still fully alive, especially in the country. The *skilly wife* was a woman who possessed the skill of curing the sick. This was seen as something intuitive, not a matter of formal education, but something which needed a person of the right cast of mind; to these innate powers learning could be gained from an older person of skill. Sometimes a man might have these abilities: 'The gardener was the skillyman of his district; deeply learned in the virtues of simples, and often applied to when the operation of blood-letting was being performed' (1814). *Simples* were herbs, and a gardener would by his trade have a deep familiarity with them.

Some had the gift of staunching the flow of blood by a phrase, but it needed the name of the injured person. There is a story of a boy in Wester Ross who suffered a wound that bled despite the use of the most powerful incantation – then someone remembered that his parentage had been disputed; the charm was repeated using the name of his real father, and all was well. A typical charm was given by a spaewife in Kirkmichael on the Water of Ae, on the southern edge of the Lowther Hills. She put a toad-shaped stone on the wound and said:

> The water's mud, an rins afluid,
> An sae dis thy bluid.
> God bid it stan, an so it did.
> In the name o' the Father, Son, an Holy Ghost
> Stan Bluid.

Another wise woman was the elderly Nanse Birrel, 'a distillator of herbs, and well skilled in the healing of sores, who had a great repute among the quarriers and colliers', who appears in John Galt's novel *Annals of the Parish* (1822). Ironically, she was found drowned in a physic well, in 1766.

Rickets is now known to be a vitamin-deficiency disease, caused by a lack of vitamin D. Here is a cure for it which was used in mid-Victorian Banffshire:

The child is taken before sunrise to a smithy in which 3 men, bearing the same name, work. One of the smiths takes the child, first lays it in the water-trough of the smithy, and then on the anvil. While lying on the anvil all the tools are, one by one, passed over the child, and the use of each is asked of the child. The nurse again receives the child and again washes it in the water-trough.

In Orkney, rickets was treated by drinking a snail and its shell dissolved in vinegar, and in Shetland oil from the *gulsa whelk*, the common snail, was used for jaundice. *Gulsa* or *gulsoch* was the name for jaundice and the herb which cured it was *gulsa girse*, jaundice grass.

The leading student of folk medicine in Scotland was David Rorie (1867-1945) who worked as a doctor in Fife and for 28 years at Cults in Aberdeenshire. At the same time as being aware of the danger of unskilled treatment, he was also fascinated by the beliefs on which traditional medicine was based. Rorie studied

Henry Law, bonesetter at Portmoak, Kinross-shire, about 1910. SLA

the work of bonesetters and criticized them not out of prejudice, but with knowledge. He understood how they imposed themselves upon, and took money from, poor people, and he was also familiar with the vast extent of their ignorance. Many bonesetters were blacksmiths:

> their skill ... is devoted to the lower disorders of the lower orders, to the relief of those who, as the Kincardineshire ploughman euphemistically described it, are 'a' wrang doon aboot the doon-aboots.'

Rorie had great sympathy for folk traditions, but he knew how much actual harm the bonesetter could do, delaying an injured man's call for a doctor, sometimes maiming him:

> A medical man may study anatomy and surgery for years, he may practice with success as a howdie or a pill-giver, but 'a' body kens doctors ken naethin' aboot banes.' And so hey! for the horny-handed hammer-holder when an injured limb cries out for real heaven-given unadulterated skill.

Folk medicine was still fully alive in the twentieth century. Nan Bain of Gairloch, Wester Ross, writing in the 1920s, explained that:

> If some one had shingles, a request went round the houses for the loan of either a black cockerel or a black cat, there must not be as much as a spot of any other colour in either the one or the other. Then blood was drawn of the cock's comb or the cat's ear, and applied to the affected parts. I remember once back in 1922 meeting a farmer walking home from a farm about 5 miles from his own and carrying a black cock under his arm. Laughingly I said, 'Where in the world did you get that moth eaten bird?' He then told me that his neighbour had shingles, and the cock was there till its comb was almost cut away to nothing, and his friend had fully recovered.

The Medical Act of 1858 had required that doctors were properly qualified: the age of the charlatan in the city was passing. But the informal practitioner in the country lived on, and some did some good with their knowledge of plants or childbirth. It was only in the period between the two World Wars that traditional folk medicine became of marginal importance. It was ended not by the rational arguments of modern medicine, but by the expansion of its power to cure, and by the presence of doctors and nurses throughout the country.

10 Other skills

Many tradesmen, particularly druggists and surgical instrument makers, supported the work of the medical profession. These men had lives and careers of their own, and often they possessed particular knowledge and unusual skills. Today almost all medical goods are made in factories: in Victorian Scotland they were made in the back shop. Like physicians and surgeons, the medical tradesmen in Edinburgh were concentrated in the streets round the Infirmary and the classrooms of the University and Surgeon's Square.

The cutler was a skilled worker in metal. He made cutlery for the table, and also specialized knives for other craftsmen – the butcher, saddler, shoemaker, and so on. The surgical cutler had to produce a large range of instruments, from amputation knives which could be sharpened to a keen edge, to dental forceps. The two Edinburgh leading firms in Edinburgh were those of Young and Gardner. The first Archibald Young set up as a cutler at the head of Leith Wynd in 1804. In 1819 his son shrewdly opened premises beside the medical school. He achieved the title of 'cutler to his Majesty' in 1832: it was not yet possible for an ambitious tradesman to make a living from surgical instrument making alone. That stage was reached in the 1880s, and for nearly a hundred years Youngs made and sold surgical instruments, bandages and artificial limbs. When the new Edinburgh Royal Infirmary and Medical School developed adjacent to one another, Youngs moved to be beside them. So did James Gardner, who had begun in business in 1866.

Perhaps the most central and long-lived idea in medicine is balance within the body. It was central to folk medicine, to Greek medicine and to the latest theories of the seventeenth century – though they differed as to the nature of the entities which were to be kept in balance, the ill effects of losing it, and the methods of restoring it. All, however, had a place for bloodletting. It was often done by barbers: their red and white pole represents blood and bandages. In some other cultures the pattern of astrological influences were important, affecting the timing of bloddletting and the quantity of blood drawn from the vein. In retrospect, we can see that there was no benefit, and that an undernourished patient would have been seriously weakened by it. It was still employed in the second half of the nineteenth century: some traditions are remarkably tenacious. Over the centuries the surgical instrument which was made in the largest numbers was the lancet, the simplest means of opening a vein.

Bloodletting was also done by leeches, and by the 1840s they were in sufficient demand for a specialist dealer in Edinburgh, the Swedish Leech Depot, to advertise:

> The Leech Depot, established since the Penny Postage by J. Wood & Co., Original Importers and Wholesale dealers in Swedish Leeches, which they import, weekly, packed in the turf they were bred in, to preserve their *health* and *quality*, which is so *superior* to any other *Leech*, that its bite inflames not, or ever leaves mark on the skin.

In the Victorian era, professors and students were clustered in the same area of Edinburgh. This was an extraordinary district of lecture rooms, lodgings, booksellers, bandage-makers, bird-stuffers, mineral dealers, anatomical theatres where corpses were dissected, and museums. There were also collections of live animals which, as was said at the time:

> on ceasing their physiological functions, obtained the obsequies of the scalpel, the injecting syringe, the spirit-jar, or macerating-tub … skins and crania for conservation might be seen hanging like banners on the outward wall or attic's roof.

William Wilson, 'Mortar Willie', in 1815.

The Apothecary drew his supply of raw materials from the fields and from wholesalers first in Amsterdam, later in London. He needed his own knowledge, contacts with whom to trade, and men to carry out the tedious work of pulverizing ingredients and mixing compounds.

The first unskilled worker to emerge before us as an individual is William Wilson, otherwise 'Mortar Willie', who came from Perthshire and said he had been in the army during the '45 and subsequently fought in Germany. He died in 1815 at the supposed age of 105: probably he lived into his late eighties. Until the end he was employed to crush dried herbs and other medicines, relentless hard work often made unpleasant by the clouds of fine dust he generated. Willie laboured for various apothecaries, and his last master continued to pay him after his strength had gone.

Pharmacy began as a craft and became an industry. The firm of T & H Smith was founded by Thomas Smith (1807-93) in 1827. His brother Henry joined him in 1836. Thomas Smith had an unusual career. He was a university-trained surgeon but he worked as a pharmacist in Edinburgh. After his work during a cholera epidemic he was paid an honorarium: with this capital he opened a shop in the New Town. Soon the manufacture of drugs became more important than the shop, and the Smiths specialized in alkaloids. They flourished because their chemical manipulations used large quantities of alcohol, which was taxed at a lower rate in Scotland than in England. In 1952 the firm bought one of its chief competitors, Duncan, Flockhart – who had made chloroform for J Y Simpson – and in 1960 they amalgamated with a third Edinburgh firm, J F Macfarlan. They are still in business.

There was a huge gulf between the Smiths and the local chemist, whose stock was described by David Rorie:

Noo droggie had an awfu' stock
Tobacco, wreetin' paper, rock ...
The best cod liver ile emulsions,
Wee poothers that could cure convulsions,
Famed Peter Puffer's soothin' syrup,
An' stuff to gar canaries chirrup.

The *droggie* was the chemist himself, named after his wares. People were often sceptical of the effect of medicines and medical men: 'Nane o' the droughery or the roguery o' doctors for me.'

Macnaughton & Son were typical chemists trading in Aberfeldy in Perthshire from 1882 to 1972. The firm was started by the son of a local merchant. In its 90 years it was run by Henry B Macnaughton and his son. Medicines are today sold chiefly as factory-made pills, tablets or capsules. In the nineteenth century and for most of the twentieth, however, chemists held a stock of raw materials which they would compound according to the doctor's prescription. Solids were ground to a powder with mortar and pestle. Some powders were made up in cachets, soluble rice envelopes. Pills were rolled using a simple machine, and for wealthier customers they were given a silver coating to enhance their appearance. All of this was done in the shop.

By the end of the nineteenth century the technology of medicine was developing rapidly. X-rays were discovered in 1895. Soon they were widely used to take photographs of broken bones and other medical conditions. Tubes were difficult to make: one craftsman described them as 'thin envelopes of glass entirely surrounded by cursing'. The skills needed were new to the medical world, and the tubes were not made in Edinburgh. Instead, shops became merely vendors of X-ray tubes made by craftsmen in factories. By 1920 this was also true of other medical goods.

11 The food of the Scots

The Scots diet of the Middle Ages was threadbare. Improved farming methods slowly created more food and in the eighteenth century country people had quite a healthy intake of food, based on kale, buttermilk and oatmeal, eaten mostly as porridge. Scots army recruits were praised for their size and good health. The Royal Infirmary in Glasgow set down the food that was to be given to patients on each day of the week. Breakfast and supper were always oatmeal porridge, except that on Sunday supper was meat broth. Dinner, eaten in the middle of the day, was meat and vegetable broth on alternate days: on two days there was herring, on another two cheese. This was a simple and nutritious pattern of eating. Only the wealthy could by overeating achieve an unhealthy diet. 'Sir, you are digging your grave with your teeth', said a physician to a corpulent patient.

The picture changed rapidly with the growth of the industrial cities, particularly Glasgow. In grinding poverty the cheapest food had to be eaten, and by the second half of the nineteenth century the importation of cheap wheat meant that many lived on bread and tea. Energy was supplied by syrup and various pre-served fruits, in the form of the *jeelie piece*. Where Cornishmen carried pasties containing potato and meat, the Scots workman carried his piece – and children in tenement back courts had them thrown down from upper windows. The *jeelie piece* does, at least, have structural stability. The transport system was not organized to deliver perishable goods such as milk, fish, vegetables and fruit to the cities in quantity: these would have enhanced the diet. In addition, the overcrowded slum flat was not the environment which an enjoyment of cooking was going to develop; many, indeed, did not have a kitchen or even a stove.

These were factors which affected Glasgow. There were larger issues which affected all of the Scots and to a large extent the Irish, who after 1840 were flooding into the west of Scotland, too. Both were poor countries in which food had rarely been a subject of interest as it had become among the peasants of France and Italy. For example, mushrooms were scarcely eaten in Scotland. The food of the urban poor was monotonous.

The diet of country people was healthier. Oatmeal, barley and dairy produce were commonly eaten in the country but not in the cities, and eggs were generally available. Many plants had been used to make food and drink. Wild carrot seeds were used instead of hops in brewing in the Hebrides. Yet even in the countryside, fruit and vegetables were eaten only in small quantities. In the towns the slow sale of vegetables led some shopkeepers to improve their greenness with copper sulphate. The City Analyst took appropriate action.

The quantity of sugar being consumed rose five-fold between the 1830s and 1930s, increasing tooth decay and becoming a substitute for healthier sources of energy. White bread, which has

One of the steps which reduced infant mortality: Glasgow Corporation supplied milk from their depot near the Saltmarket, 1906-7.

DO YOU REALISE
THAT THE
Glasgow Poor Children's
Fresh-Air Fortnight
HAVE HOMES OPEN
ALL THE YEAR ROUND
AT
BIGGART HOSPITAL HOME, PRESTWICK,
ASHGROVE HOME, MAYBOLE
(Convalescent Home),
ROCKVALE CHILD WELFARE HOME,
SALTCOATS.
WILL YOU HELP
TO
HELP THE HELPLESS?
NO COLLECTORS ARE EMPLOYED.
The Annual Requirements now amount to
Over £15,000.
Send your Donations to the Hon. Treasurer,
WILLIAM HUTSON, M.A., B.L.,
82 MITCHELL STREET, GLASGOW, C.I.

The Fresh-Air Fortnight was a charity which aimed to give poor children a holiday away from Glasgow's intensely polluted atmosphere, and to feed them properly for two weeks. This advertisement dates from 1923.

many of the important nutrients in flour removed, became common even in remote glens. Burnett's Inverness Steam Bakery claimed to supply white bread to the Highlands. The more expensive form was the pan loaf: thus a *pan loaf accent* came from Morningside or Kelvinside. Yet the poor had the more nutritious bread.

The effects of the Scottish industrial diet were suddenly revealed in 1899-1902 when during the Boer War potential army recruits were examined. In some areas of the West of Scotland half were rejected. There was a national outcry: it was as though the British people had themselves decayed. And if the result was that it was difficult to win a small war in South Africa, what would be the nation's fate in a larger conflict? Diet thus met politics, and scientists began to unravel the facts.

Rickets was a curse in Glasgow, producing the characteristic stunted and bowly-legged adult. It was caused by a deficiency of vitamin D and calcium, due to poor diet and a lack of sunlight under the pall of smoke which hung above the city. Once the causes had been identified – vitamins were discovered in the early 1920s – simple action reduced the number of new cases. Sufferers were still often seen in the streets of Glasgow in the 1960s.

A soup kitchen in Vale of Leven, Dunbartonshire, in the 1930s. By the Depression it was understood that a healthy diet included not only fat, protein and carbohydrate, but also minerals and vitamins. SLA

The link between poverty and poor food and health was proved beyond doubt by John Boyd Orr in his book *Food, Health and Income* in 1936. During the Second World War the Scots people, and children in particular, had a better diet than ever before. Rationing was essential, and the Treasury proposed that it should be done simply by price. Nutritionists, particularly Boyd Orr, successfully argued that food supplies could be controlled so that as well as ensuring that everyone had enough to eat, the balance of the diet was improved. White bread had been made from highly-milled flour which had thirty per cent of its mass and much of its goodness removed. In wartime the 'extraction rate' was raised and the bread was more 'wholesome' if a strange grey-brown colour. Real white bread did not reappear until 1953.

12 Medicine and all of the people

'I was a stranger and ye took me in, I was sick and ye visited me.' This is the inspiring text over the door of Edinburgh Royal Infirmary. Christ used these words to say that those who gave to charity were also giving to him. They make a historical point, because most large hospitals were 'voluntary': they were paid for by charity and by the patients' fees. One of the most important themes in medicine in the first half of the twentieth century is the growth of the idea that every individual has a right to adequate medical care.

In the aftermath of the 1745 rebellion the government's view of the Highlands and Islands of Scotland was that they had to be controlled and their distinctive culture suppressed. When it was clear that control had been achieved, the government thought little of them, though it was grateful for the flow of recruits for the army – many of them men who could not be supported by the land. Yet the north and west of Scotland had distinctive health problems, and there was a famine in some areas of Scotland at the same time as the Great Hunger in Ireland.

By 1900 medical provision in the Highlands and Islands was far behind the rest of Britain. There were few doctors, and those who

*Nurses in everyday clothes at the newly-completed
Chalmers Hospital, Banff, about 1864. They are holding
symbols of their work, one copying Florence Nightingale,
'the Lady with the Lamp'. The man is probably a builder.*

did work in the Highlands endured a low income and high travelling expenses. In the Lowlands, the minister and the doctor had a similar status: in the Highlands the minister was far wealthier.

The difficulties of the situation were highlighted after the government introduced the National Insurance scheme in 1911. It assumed that people earned wages and lived in a cash economy, but crofters provided their own food by farming and fishing, and otherwise lived largely by barter. When the government recognized the problem they set up a committee which produced a far-seeing report in 1912, recommending minimum salaries for doctors, the provision of nurses, and a programme of hospital building. This was a far greater level of state support for medicine than any proceeding one, yet some funds were found for it and

*Dr Lachlan Grant in Glencoe village, Argyllshire, about
1900, vaccinating a baby against smallpox. He was also
the local dentist and optician.* SLA

the Highlands and Islands Medical Service (HIMS) was set in
place.

The First World War and the depression of the 1920s delayed
the full implementation of HIMS, but the number and quality of
doctors rose quickly. In the 1930s a building programme produced new or extended hospitals at Stornoway, Fort William,
Golspie, Wick and Lerwick. A novel feature of medical provision
in the islands was the Air Ambulance, which first flew in 1935.

Even in the cities, the medical profession had only limited
contact with the poor. For example, childbirth in the home was
usual, but doctors would not go into the worst slum areas – so it
was left to medical students. Each one had to deliver a dozen
babies before qualification and every Glasgow medical autobiog-
raphy contains stories of this vivid experience: of neighbours,
women far more familiar with childbirth, taking charge; of anaesthetic ether being employed to still large beetles running over the

bed; of dark and unlit closes where the sight of the doctor's black bag was the best protection against assault.

The Second World War saw notable improvements in the health of Scotland, and its health services. In 1939 it was recognized that if there were heavy military casualties on the Continent, perhaps accompanied by a large number of people injured by bombing in south-east England, then the wounded would be best treated well away from the conflict – in Scotland. So new hospitals were built outside towns, and this is the reason for the apparently odd location of some, such as Peel Hospital, in the Tweed Valley four miles from Galashiels, Stracathro in the Angus countryside

Nurses with wounded soldiers at a military hospital during the First World War. The location is unknown, but is probably a country mansion requisitioned for this purpose. SLA

The final year class at Edinburgh University Medical School in 1911: four professors, four women, and 108 men students.

and Raigmore outside Inverness. The anticipated casualties did not appear, and so the facilities were opened to local people involved with the war effort and then to almost everyone.

The National Health Service came into being on 5 July 1948. The NHS took over 64,000 beds in voluntary and local-authority hospitals. Ten years later only one new hospital had been built, at Vale of Leven in Dunbartonshire. A programme of construction then began. In addition many of the smaller hospitals were closed: by 1991 there were only 52,000 beds. The pattern of medical provision changed: specialist services instead of being concentrated in the teaching hospitals were spread more widely. By 1980 the NHS had 150,000 staff in Scotland, one in fifteen of those at work.

The spread of medical services to the whole population was mirrored by the access of the whole population to all medical roles: women fought their way into the medical profession. The first woman to be admitted to study medicine at a Scottish university was Sophia Jex-Blake (1840-1912) in 1869. Opposition to women doctors grew rapidly, and she took her degree in Switzerland. Some of the Edinburgh professors were strongly prejudiced, as were many of the male students. One of the women's few supporters was the sharp-edged personality of Professor John Hughes Bennett who already disagreed with his colleagues on other topics – perhaps not a helpful ally. There was intense competition for posts and young men did not welcome the idea

Dr Elsie Inglis (1864-1917) in Serbian uniform.

of able young women taking jobs from them. Many also were unhappy at the idea of a woman doctor examining a man's body.

Jex-Blake set up a series of institutions in Edinburgh: a dispensary for women and children in 1878, and seven years later the first hospital in Scotland to be run by and for women. As well as performing the usual functions of a small hospital it also acted as a haven for the overworked and undernourished. When it closed a hundred years later, only this hospital and one in London had resisted the appointment of male staff. Jex-Blake also created her own medical school in Edinburgh and by the 1890s the universities altered their regulations so that women could study and qualify in medicine. She was a determined woman but not a comfortable personality: one of her pupils, Elsie Inglis (1864-1917), organized another medical school.

By 1914 the idea of women studying and practising medicine was established. For example, about ten per cent of Glasgow medical graduates were women, a total of 187 between 1894 and 1914. There were difficulties, however: many hospitals refused to appoint women, male practitioners were often hostile, and

Edinburgh did not admit women to university medical classes until the First World War. At the beginning of the War Elsie Inglis offered to organize hospitals staffed by women: when the British government declined, the offer was repeated to other governments, and several accepted. Women thus showed that their work was fully professional, and some of the bias against them had gone by 1939. As in other professions, women are still under-represented in senior positions. For example, at Glasgow University the first woman medical professor was not appointed until the late 1970s.

13 Epidemics, antibiotics and numbers

A traveller wrote of the people of Orkney and Shetland, 'They have a charm whereby they try if persons be in a decay or not, and if they will die thereof.' *Decay* did not indicate a general feebleness or physical decline: it was a specific disease which later became known as consumption and then as pulmonary tuberculosis. But as with other diseases, it was not understood to have specific causes and symptoms. In 1792 it was said that at Edzell in Angus common illnesses were the result of 'poor diet, hard labour, and sorry lodging'. In time, understanding increased. Tuberculosis had always been present, but it did not become a matter of central importance until other diseases such as smallpox and typhoid were coming under control. By 1900 it was 'the question of the day'. At this point a meeting was held in London to discuss the idea of a crusade against tuberculosis. The Prince of Wales, later King Edward VII was present: not an intellectual, not a man inclined to make a question more complex than it had to be. He asked, 'if preventable why not prevented?' and the campaign moved forward.

Tuberculosis was almost wiped out in the forty years after the Second World War. A mass X-ray campaign allowed much earlier diagnosis, and antibiotics could defeat it. But the story did not end there for tuberculosis was not finally conquered and it

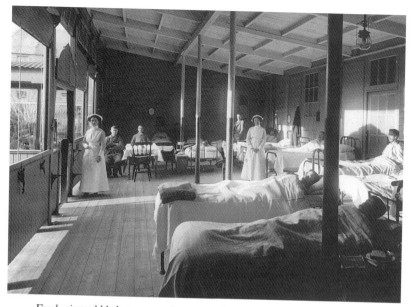

Fresh air could help to cure pulmonary tuberculosis, and wealthy sufferers went to the Alps. Patients at Greenlea Poorhouse, Edinburgh, had their beds in open pavilions, about 1910.

survived especially in Third World countries, partly because wealthier nations did not choose to support the medical work which would have eradicated it. At the same time the bacillus was evolving so that it became increasingly resistant to drugs. In 1993 the World Health Organization declared it a global emergency, for it was killing more adults than any other infectious disease.

Influenza is a highly contagious viral disease. Its ability to strike a large area quickly led in Italy to the idea that it was caused by the stars, by the 'influence'. Its pandemics are awesome. That of 1889-90 probably affected half of the population of the world, and that of 1918-9 swept the world as the First World War was ending and killed well over 20 million in six months – more than had died in war.

A pharmacist in Aberfeldy in Perthshire remembered how hard he had worked:

> Starting at 8.30 a.m., customers who presented prescriptions in person had them made up while they waited. All frills, such as capping and wrapping of bottles, were discontinued. [Each took half an hour for lunch] then it was back to work till tea-time, when a hurried meal was snatched in preparation for the evening rush. At 7.00 p.m. the doors were closed, but the work went on; when the customers were all disposed of, it was time to tackle the sheaf of prescriptions which had been handed in by the doctors. When these had been made up, the two overworked chemists divided the town into two areas to deliver the medicines to the stricken homes. Miraculously, neither of them was struck down by the 'flu.

The success of aseptic surgery, and the use of old antiseptics such as hydrogen peroxide and new ones such as TCP and Dettol, showed that bacteria in the open could be killed. But bacteria inside the body could not be treated with these power-ful, blunt weapons, and the search began for chemicals which would attack only the disease-causing bacteria, leaving all other cells alone. This was done by starting from a chemical which had promising properties, and synthesizing hundreds of similar ones. The search for the 'magic bullet' achieved its first success with the 606th compound examined by Paul Ehrlich in Frankfurt in 1909.

The next development, the discovery of antibiotics, was of even greater importance. Antibiotics are substances produced by living organisms which are capable of destroying or inhibiting the growth of micro-organisms. Alexander Fleming was born at Darvel in Ayrshire, trained at St Mary's Hospital in London and worked there all his life. He discovered the powerful antibiotic effect of penicillin in 1928. Yet it was difficult to produce, unsta-ble, and difficult to use. These problems were solved by a team in Oxford in 1940-1, and the American pharmaceutical industry urgently sought ways of expanding production. When the Allied armies landed in Normandy in the summer of 1944 there was sufficient penicillin to treat all the serious casualties. Soon other antibiotics were discovered: streptomycin (1944), for example, when combined with other drugs, cured all but the most advanced cases of tuberculosis.

When in 1788 King George III's mind collapsed the government was faced by a problem for which there was no precedent: what to do with a mad head of state? Soon a specific question emerged: what was his chance of recovery? What, in general, was the proportion of people with any illness who could be cured? None of the King's physicians had

Marie Warren, a laboratory assistant, measuring the sugar content of cerebrospinal fluid, about 1955. SLA

any idea: they treated the individual patient, not the populace, and most respectable doctors held madness at a distance. Dr William Black, a Scot trained in Edinburgh, had quietly investigated the question and he gave a disturbing answer: one third of psychiatric patients recover completely, another third partially, and the remainder remain impaired. But in which class was the King? There was no way of knowing.

William Black's work was one of the starting points for the study of the statistics of disease – epidemiology. Another was the practice of compiling 'bills of mortality' which showed the causes of death in a city over a year. The use of numbers was essential to the development of public health in the nineteenth century. In a different way, it also related to the use of diagnostic instruments, such as the thermometer, which produced numbers, or graphs, or imaging techniques which are based on numerical computation.

14 Medicine, physics and technology

The eighteenth-century physician made his diagnosis by asking the patient to describe the development of his symptoms. The body itself was rarely examined beyond a check of the pulse. Thus there was little interest in increasing the sensitivity of the five senses, or in measuring the properties of the body. When suitable instruments were invented, they were largely ignored.

The first man to make thermometers which were both accurate and sensitive was Daniel Gabriel Fahrenheit (1686-1736), who was born in Danzig but worked in Amsterdam. His work was admired by a Scots medical student at Leiden, George Martine (1702-41) of St Andrews. Martine failed to be chosen as one of the medical professors at Edinburgh in 1726, so he returned to his birthplace, practised as a physician and investigated the role of body heat in physiology. His house still stands in South Street.

Martine needed thermometers, and was fortunate to find someone in St Andrews with the very high degree of manual skill needed to reproduce Fahrenheit's work. Alexander Wilson (1714-86) later achieved fame as the type founder who made possible the elegant printing of the Foulis brothers in Glasgow. Wilson's thermometers were so fragile that he had to enclose them in a glass sheath, so they took a long time to reach a steady temperature. Martine recorded that he had studied the body temperature of the honey bee by holding a thermometer in the middle of a swarm for twenty minutes. Wilson's thermometers later became vital to Joseph Black's studies of the nature of heat. Nevertheless the clinical thermometer, today found in every family medicine cabinet, was not to become a part of the apparatus of diagnosis until the second half of the nineteenth century.

The sphygmograph, which produced a graph of the variation in the blood pressure in an artery, was one of the new instruments of that period. Its inventor gave a caustic description of the traditional doctor:

> he concentrated his attention mainly on the pulse, in the feeling of which there was always scope for affecting the possession of peculiar

skill and insight. To the uninitiated, who regard the doctor as the depository of occult knowledge, there was something very imposing in his method of pulse-palpitation. The fingers of the right hand daintily grasping the patient's wrist, while the doctor's eyes were riveted on the loud-ticking gold chronometer he held in his left hand, his head gravely nodding the while synchronously with the arterial pulsations – all this formed a picture calculated to inspire beholders with reverence and awe.

Dr John Spence (1871-1930), pioneer radiologist. He is hiding his mutilated right arm.

This is polemical, for a skilled physician could learn much from the pulse. Yet science had solved many important medical problems and many believed that it could solve all. By the end of the nineteenth century scientific instruments were a part of medicine. John McKendrick, professor of physiology at Glasgow from 1876, told a story against his predecessor:

> one day he showed his class a large modern microscope, all bright, beautiful brass work, with mysterious screws and a moveable stage ... he added, 'Look at it, gentlemen, but do not touch it,' An irreverent voice came from a back bench, 'Then what the devil did you bring it here for?'

The use of instruments had hitherto increased slowly: the young believed in them, the elderly were more cautious. Now something dramatic happened. At the end of 1895, Wilhelm Conrad Röntgen discovered X-rays. He posted the announcement of his results from Würzburg on 30 December, and by the end of the first week of January 1896 X-rays were known all over the world

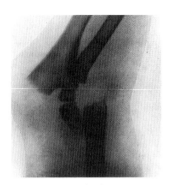

One of the first X-ray images produced in Scotland, showing the elbow joint, 1897-8.

and every newspaper speculated on their possible use. The medical importance of X-rays was immediately understood: few discoveries have become known all over the world so quickly. Within a few weeks several doctors in Scotland were experimenting with the new rays.

Dawson Turner (1857-1929) was the first in Edinburgh. In the early years the harmful effects of large doses, and of repeated doses, were not understood. Turner, like many X-ray pioneers, suffered severely in later life from dermatitis caused by the rays. One of his pupils was John Spence (1871-1930), the radiologist at the Royal Edinburgh Hospital for Sick Children from 1907. Spence's medical knowledge was matched by his personality: 'He had a fascinating power over children frightened by the darkness of the X-ray room (in former days), and by the cracking and sparking of the electric current. At these times he seemed to know every charm against fear – sympathy, bantering, even a little scolding – and he knew how to mix those ingredients in the charm, so that the child submitted quietly and confidently to the ordeal.' Spence, like other pioneers, suffered dreadfully from over-exposure to X-rays. Fingers had to be amputated, then his right arm, then parts of his left hand. The Carnegie Hero Fund Trust recognized his unselfishness and sacrifice with the award of a medal and an annuity. Spence continued to work, paying out of the annuity the salary of the assistant he needed to manipulate patients.

Turner's counterpart in Glasgow was John Macintyre (1857-1928), a surgeon. The first public showing of a ciné film took place in the same week as Röntgen announced X-rays: Macintyre combined the two new technologies. His first film is said to have been of the bones of a housemaid's knee. The earliest to survive is of a frog's leg: it is the oldest cineradiograph (1897).

Radiology was successful, particularly in detecting fractures, and it developed rapidly during the First World War. It soon became expensive and demanding in other ways. It needed a reliable supply of electricity from which a large current could be drawn. One hospital, proud of its new electric lift, found that it could not be used when a radiograph was being taken. At Huntly in Aberdeenshire the

Unloading bottles from the blood-plasma freeze-dryer, Edinburgh, about 1950.

power came from a local woollen mill which had to be warned of the impending use of the X-ray apparatus because it affected the mill's machinery.

One of the consequences of vastly increased medical knowledge in the twentieth century is that the medical world has itself become much more complex. More procedures require more equipment – but also administrative structures and funding. At the end of the century, novelty is expected and it is assumed that change will have to be managed. Earlier, change sometimes produced unusual situations. Take the introduction of blood transfusion. Various trials of transfusion had been made from the seventeenth to the nineteenth centuries, but it was only in 1900 that the existence of different blood groups was discovered in Germany. Even then, transfusion was rare: only a few hundred patients were so treated during the carnage of the First World War. Transfusion was directly from donor to patient: the two had to lie side by side.

In 1929 a woman bled to death in Edinburgh because no blood donor was available. Her husband told a friend, a dentist called Jack Copland, who was moved to involve a Christian group, the

Crusaders, to create a pool of donors and raise funds. In 1931, 20 transfusions were performed in the City; in 1937, 560. The Civil War in Spain began in 1936 and blood banks were developed successfully there: blood could be stored until it was needed. The first in Scotland was set up less than a week before the start of the Second World War. Research in Cambridge showed how blood plasma could be freeze-dried, and equipment was brought into use in Edinburgh in 1943. As Dr Alastair Masson explained:

> The drying plant was in a basement in the Royal Infirmary – officially 'in underground premises safe from air raid risks', unofficially in a 'small unventilated cellar'. The refrigerator for the unit was installed at a cost of £530, paid for by a remarkably generous gift from the pupils and staff of the Mary Erskine School for Girls, then called Edinburgh Ladies' College. The plant had a capacity of one hundred bottles in a length of steel pipe ('large diameter city water supply pipe'). The refrigerant was methyl chloride which was both toxic and inflammable. The plant ran day and night for years, serviced devotedly by the senior technician, Andrew Crosbie. That unit put Edinburgh in the forefront of blood transfusion technology.

Despite the immense value of the blood transfusion service officialdom resented its newness and its cost, referred to it as 'Frankenstein', and only regularized its funding in 1948. From these developments in Edinburgh grew the Scottish National Blood Transfusion Service which is still one of the world leaders in its field. Two other technical developments of great importance also took place in Scotland, in Glasgow and Aberdeen.

Ian Donald (1910-87) was Professor of Obstetrics and Gynaecology at Glasgow. One of his patients was the wife of a shipbuilder, and in 1955 Donald began to wonder whether a technique which was used for checking the quality of welding in

A scene on a flag day in Edinburgh, collecting money for the Blood Transfusion Service, about 1945.

I AM GOLDIE
THIS IS MY ...
THIRD ...

ARE YOU
BETWEEN
18 and 60
?

EDINBURGH & S.E. BLOOD TRANSFUSION SERVICE

IF YOU ARE—

HALF-AN-HOUR of YOUR TIME
WILL GIVE SOMEONE ELSE A LIFETIME

20,000 MORE DONORS NEEDED

PLEASE ENROL AT YOUR NEAREST CHEMIST
OR AT OFFICE 12 GILMORE PLACE EDINBURGH

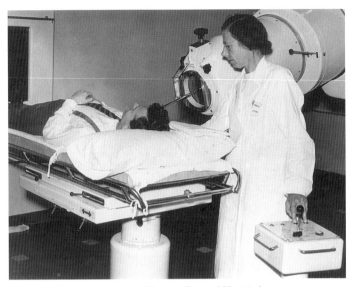

The radiotherapy unit at the Western General Hospital, Edinburgh, about 1970. SLA

ships – ultrasound – might not also reveal the difference between a foetus and a tumour or other growth in the womb. Some simple tests showed he was right. Early research into the deployment of the technique was frustrating, but in 1957 he showed that a woman who was thought to be dying of cancer of the stomach in fact had only a large ovarian cyst. 'From this point', wrote Donald, 'there could be no turning back.' The patient recovered following simple treatment; the first commercial ultrasound scanner was sold in 1961 and today almost every impending mother sees the foetus on an ultrasound monitor. Donald and his colleagues in Glasgow made many important advances in its technology and use. Donald was a physician rather than a physicist: his position as Professor of Obstetrics meant that he had access to hundreds of patients. The Queen Mother's [maternity] Hospital opened in 1964 beside the University, and a friend remembered: 'The new hospital gave full scope for Ian Donald's enthusiasms and histrionic skill. He ran it like an actor-manager of the old school, directing the productions, and playing all the leading parts himself.' He had the highest reputation as a teacher.

At the same time Professor John Mallard in Aberdeen was developing several new techniques, using modern physics to create images of the body, most often to detect and define tumours. Mallard carried out early work on the Gamma Camera. After radioactive isotopes emitting gamma rays have been injected into the body, their distribution can reveal anomalous growth: much of the difficulty of this technique, and of the sophistication of the Gamma Camera, lies in making an accurate picture. Among other diagnostic techniques, Mallard became interested in a group of phenomena relating to the behaviour of atoms which had been excited by radio waves: it led to the

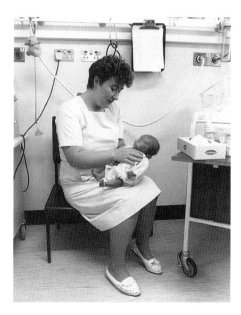

A very young patient halfway through his feed in the Special Baby Care Unit, St John's Hospital, Livingstone, 1990. SLA

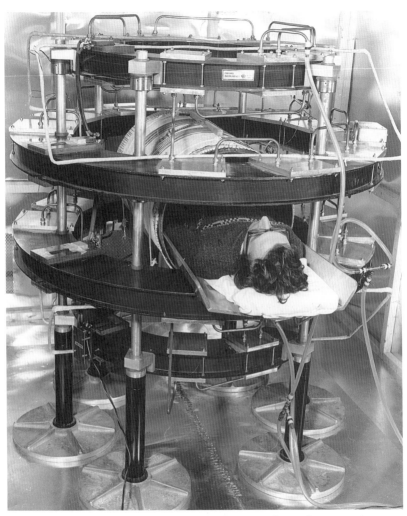

The Aberdeen Magnetic Resonance Image Scanner, 1980, the first instrument of its kind to produce an image from which a diagnosis could be made. Inside is one of the designers, Dr Jim Hutchison.

development of Magnetic Resonance Imaging (MRI). An American physician, Raymond V Damadian, had seen how powerful this technique might be, and Mallard and his team built the first MRI scanner which gave genuinely useful clinical results. Of crucial importance was application of highly sophisticated mathematics to transform the signals received from the body into an intelligible image. This was the point at which the computer entered the technology of medical diagnosis. Given the limited resources available to Mallard and his colleagues, their achievement was remarkable; but the technical lead was taken over by American and Japanese companies who had access to far larger resources of capital. This is a dismally familiar story in modern British industry.

15 The Scottishness of medicine in Scotland

Even in the late Middle Ages, Scottish medicine had a European quality: ancient writers such as Hippocrates and Galen were known, and there was an international trade in herbs and spices for medical as well as culinary purposes. Other aspects of health were distinctively Scots.

Scots words were used for many aspects of health and sickness. For example, different kinds of chest complaint have their own vocabulary. A *blocher* is a loose, catarrhal cough – 'Fat's adee wi ye that ye're aye blocherin an spittin?' – whilst a *clocher* is rough and wheezing, a *hask* short and dry, a *keuch* a persistently tickling cough, and a *bucher* a fit of uncontrollable coughing. The word *coughle*, with its diminutive ending, indicates a weak cough. To *boich* is to cough with difficulty. Whooping cough is *chincough*, *kinkcough*, *kinkhoast*, the *kinks* or the *kinkers*, and the *backdraught* is the baby's deep gasp for breath while suffering from it. 'Fin little Peter hid the kinkhoast, he wiz sometimes blue i' the face wi' the backdraugh.' (Banffshire, 1932). All of this is quite different from the healthy *pech* – the hard breath after exertion, or from being *gowstie* – breathless from being overweight.

EDINBURGH CORPORATION
PUBLIC HEALTH DEPARTMENT

TELEPHONE:
CALedonian 4471

JOHNSTON TERRACE
EDINBURGH 1

30th January, 1959

DEAR EDINBURGH HOUSEHOLDER,

As many people are seriously concerned about the danger to health from cigarette-smoking, I feel it is my duty as Medical Officer of Health of your City to tell you the facts.

There has been in recent years a very great increase in deaths from lung cancer, and many investigations in our own and other countries have shown a close relationship with tobacco-smoking. The Medical Research Council, which is, of course, our most authoritative medical opinion, has advised the Government that a major part of this increase is associated with tobacco-smoking, particularly in the form of cigarettes.

The seriousness of the position can be seen from the fact that over 21,000 people died from lung cancer in Great Britain in 1957 and this number is increasing by about 1,000 each year.

There is no safe amount of tobacco-smoking. To smoke at all means an increased risk of contracting lung cancer. The wisest policy is to give up smoking altogether. For those who cannot give it up, a reduction in the number of cigarettes smoked or, better still, a change to pipe-smoking reduces the risk but does not abolish it. **I am satisfied that the great majority of lung cancer cases would be prevented if our people would give up tobacco-smoking.**

These are the facts. The choice is yours ; but none will doubt the importance of persuading young people to avoid a habit which, once established, is so difficult to break, and which may well cause serious damage to their future health.

Yours sincerely,

H. E. Seiler.

Medical Officer of Health.

A new girl arrived at a school in the Trongate of Glasgow in 1775, and when asked whether she had suffered from any illnesses, she replied:

> Yes, mem, I've had the sma'pox, the nirls [chicken-pox], the blabs [nettle-rash], the scaw [itch], the kink-hoast [whooping-cough], the fever, the branks [mumps], and the worm [toothache].

The *nirls* were not to be confused with the *mirls* – measles or more generally any disease characterized by a rash. In the same way the *branks* or *buffets* refer to any swelling in the throat, not just mumps.

These words are less used today. This is partly due to the decline in the use of Scots, but also to greater medical precision in the use of words. Traditional language is good at describing symptoms; science needs to express underlying causes.

The group of words which described the condition of the body were as much concerned with health as with illness. *Hail and fere* was a common expression:

> An there's the minister ... awa to the curlin' in winter an' the gowfin' in simmer, as hale an' feir as ye like.

If a newly-caught fish was *lowpin an levin* it meant that it was still moving, not quite dead. Of a human being it was used ironically to mean the opposite – in the best of health.

At the head of the medical profession were the professors in the four universities, the founts of all knowledge. At the other end of the scale was the common midwife, with little formal education but sometimes with extensive experience – the *howdie*, as she was known in Scots. At Aberdeen the Professor of Midwifery was known to his disrespectful pupils as the *howdie*.

Three Scots medical men have won the Nobel Prize for Medicine. The discoverer of the malaria parasite, Ronald Ross,

The link between cigarette smoking and lung cancer was shown in 1950. SLA

was Nobel laureate in 1902: he was born in India of a Scots family. Sir Alexander Fleming won the prize in 1945 for his part in the discovery of penicillin, and Sir James Black in 1988. Black was the pharmacologist who developed beta-blockers which reduce the heart rate and the heart's force of contraction, and are widely used in the treatment of heart disease; he also devised anti-ulcer drugs. John Boyd Orr's work on poverty, diet and health has already been mentioned. After the Second World War he turned his mind to the greater problem of starvation. The use of words with a biblical tone gave weight to his pronouncement on inter-national attempts to address famine in the Third World: 'They asked for food and we gave them paper.' One can feel his anger. Boyd Orr was awarded the Nobel Prize for Peace in 1949. By coincidence, Fleming and Boyd Orr both received some of their education at Kilmarnock Academy. These men helped to give Scotland its place in world medicine.

We have seen how, by the middle of the twentieth century, one medical tradition had extinguished all others: scientific medicine, the medicine of the large hospital, was almost completely domi-nant. Since then, the situation has become far more complex. Older western traditions such as herbalism and homeopathy, have gained strength. There has been increasing interest in medical techniques from other cultures, such as acupuncture from China.

Now, approaching the millennium, there is little to distinguish the practice of medicine in Scotland from the rest of western medicine – except that it involves the Scots. The distinctive char-acter of our medicine is its need to respond to the results of our behaviour. In the 1950s it became fashionable for women to smoke: forty years later Glasgow has the highest rate of lung cancer in women *in the world*. Smoking, combined with the fatty Scots diet and our lack of enthusiasm for exercise, produces a high incidence of heart disease. We live longer lives, but not necessarily healthier ones.

FURTHER READING

There are three reliable histories of medicine in Scotland:

COMRIE, **J D**. *History of Scottish Medicine* 2 vols. 2nd ed. London 1932.

HAMILTON D. *The Healers: a history of medicine in Scotland* Edinburgh 1981.

MACLACHLAN G (ed). *Improving the Common Weal: aspects of Scottish health services 1900-1984* Edinburgh 1987.

General works on the history of medicine:

BYNUM W F and PORTER R (eds). *Companion Encyclopedia of the History of Medicine* 2 vols London 1993.

SINGER, C and UNDERWOOD, E A. *A Short History of Medicine* 2nd ed Oxford 1962.

Some works on particular aspects of medicine in Scotland and beyond, are:

ALEXANDER,W. *First Ladies of Medicine* Glasgow 1987, on Glasgow graduates.

BANNERMAN, J. *The Beatons: a medical kindred in the classical Gaelic tradition* Edinburgh 1986.

BUCHAN, D (ed). *Folk Tradition and Folk Medicine: the writings of David Rorie* Edinburgh 1994.

DARWIN, T. *The Scots Herbal: the plant lore of the Scots* Edinburgh 1996.

DAVIS, A B. *Medicine and its Technology: an introduction to the history of medical instrumentation* Westport (Conn) 1981.

DUNN,C L. *History of the Second World War: Emergency Medical Services*, 1952.

DINGWALL, H. *Physicians, Surgeons and Apothecaries: medical practice in seventeenth-century Edinburgh* Phantassie (East Lothian) 1995.

MORRIS, R and F. *Scottish Healing Wells* Sandy 1982.

REISER, S J. *Medicine and the Reign of Technology* Cambridge 1978.

Report on the Committee on the Highlands and Islands Medical Services 1912 Cd.6559.

SIMPSON, M. *Simpson, the obstetrician* London 1972, a biography of J Y Simpson.

WRIGHT-ST CLAIR, R E. *Doctors Monro: a medical saga* London 1964.

Material on diet and health can be found in:

KITCHIN, A H and PASSMORE, R. *The Scotsman's Food* Edinburgh 1949.

The Scottish Diet: report of a working party to the Chief Medical Officer for Scotland Edinburgh 1993, an important scientific report.

SCOTTISH OFFICE DEPARTMENT OF HEALTH. *Eating for Health: a diet action plan for Scotland* Edinburgh 1996.

STEVEN, M. *The Good Scots Diet* Aberdeen 1985.

ORR, J B. *Food, Health and Income* London 1936.

PLACES TO VISIT

The most important exhibition of medical history in Scotland is in the Sir Jules Thorn Gallery at the Royal College of Surgeons of Edinburgh, which is open from 2 to 4 pm from Monday to Friday. Many museums of social history and country life contain material on the Scots diet.

At the National Museums of Scotland, the new Museum of Scotland (opening November 1998) will tell the story of Scotland and will include important medical material from the eighteenth and early nineteenth centuries. The *Instruments of Science* gallery contains some objects of medical importance, including Joseph Black's glassware and nineteenth-century microscopes.

Place names sometimes indicate places of medical interest. *Liberton* occurs near Edinburgh, and *Libberton* near Biggar: they were probably leper colonies. Street names sometimes indicate the former locations of places of medical importance, as *Infirmary Street* in Edinburgh, where the city's main hospital stood until 1890.